Cute and Whimsical Elves

A Color Therapy Coloring Book

By

Kim Jordan Blair

I want to thank Robin Fiercecry Beasley for granting me permission, to use her colored version of my little elf taking a bath.

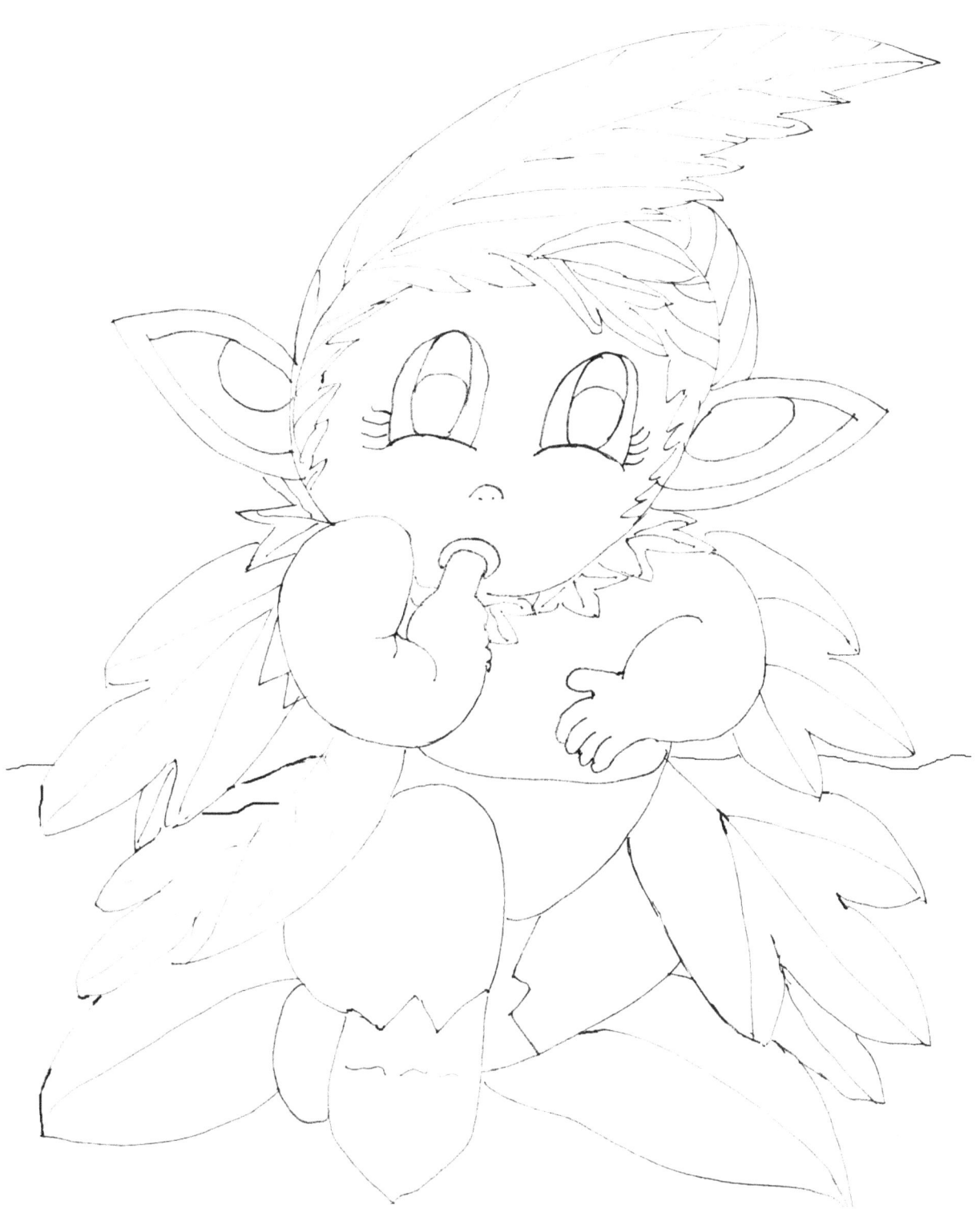

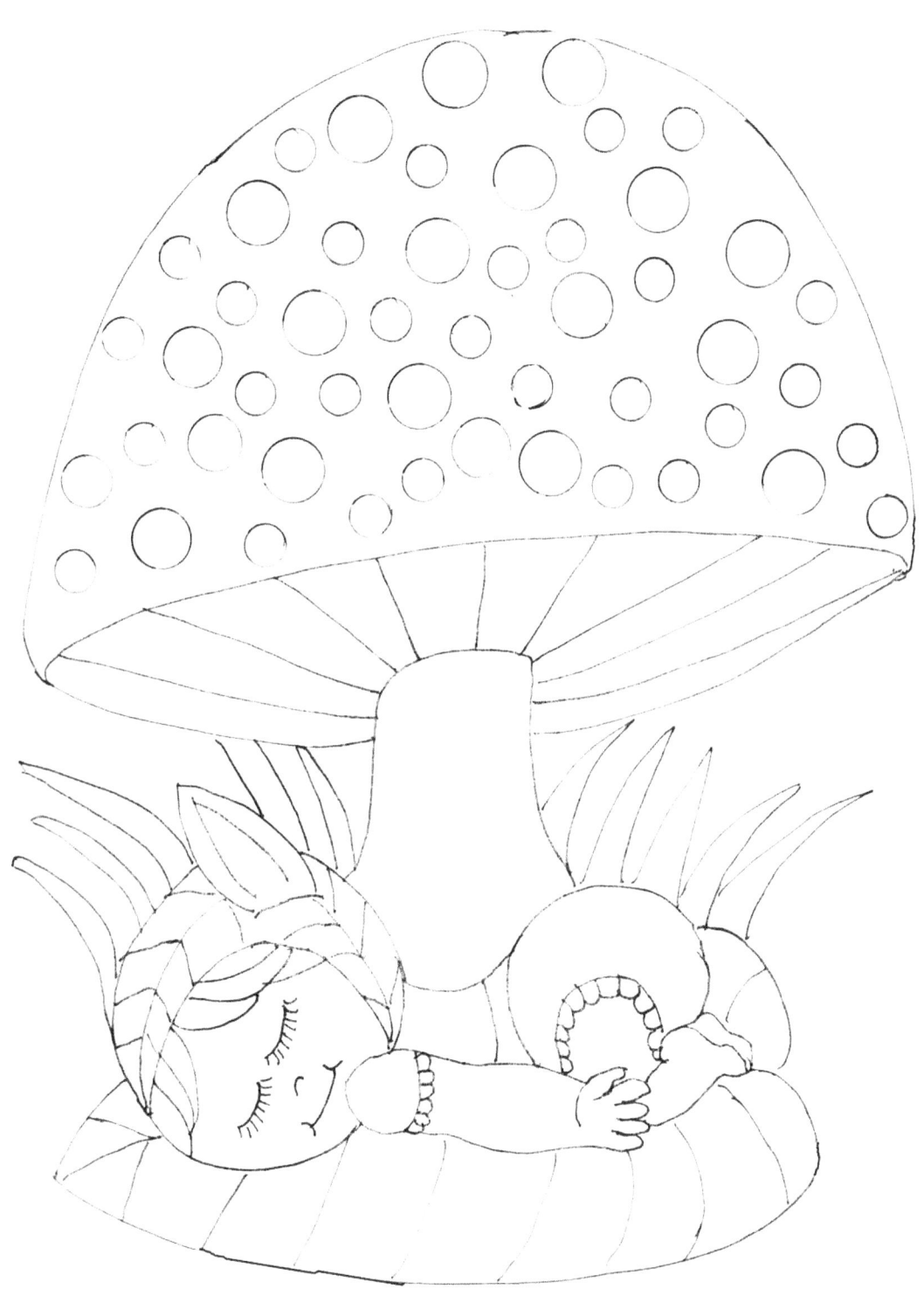

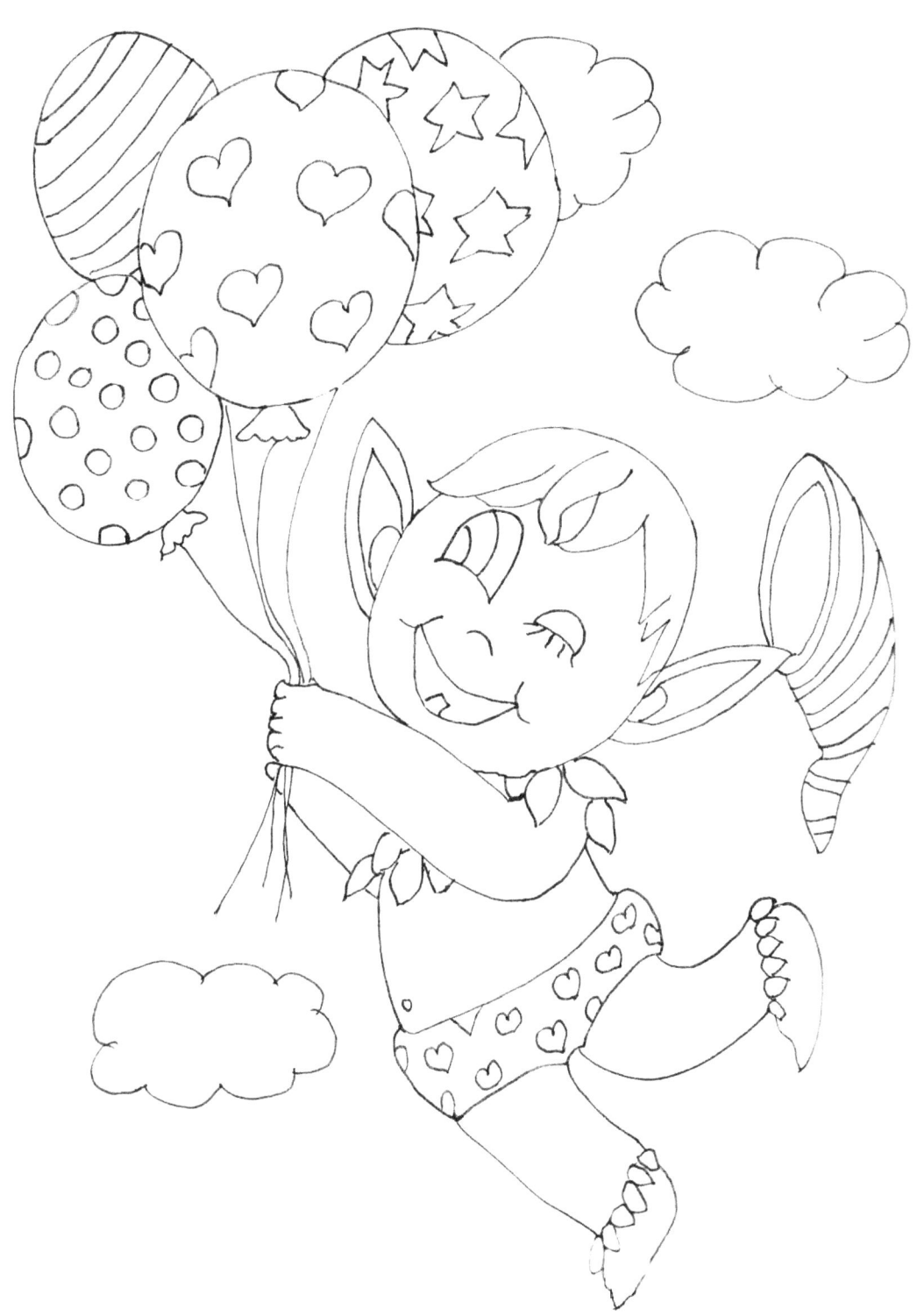

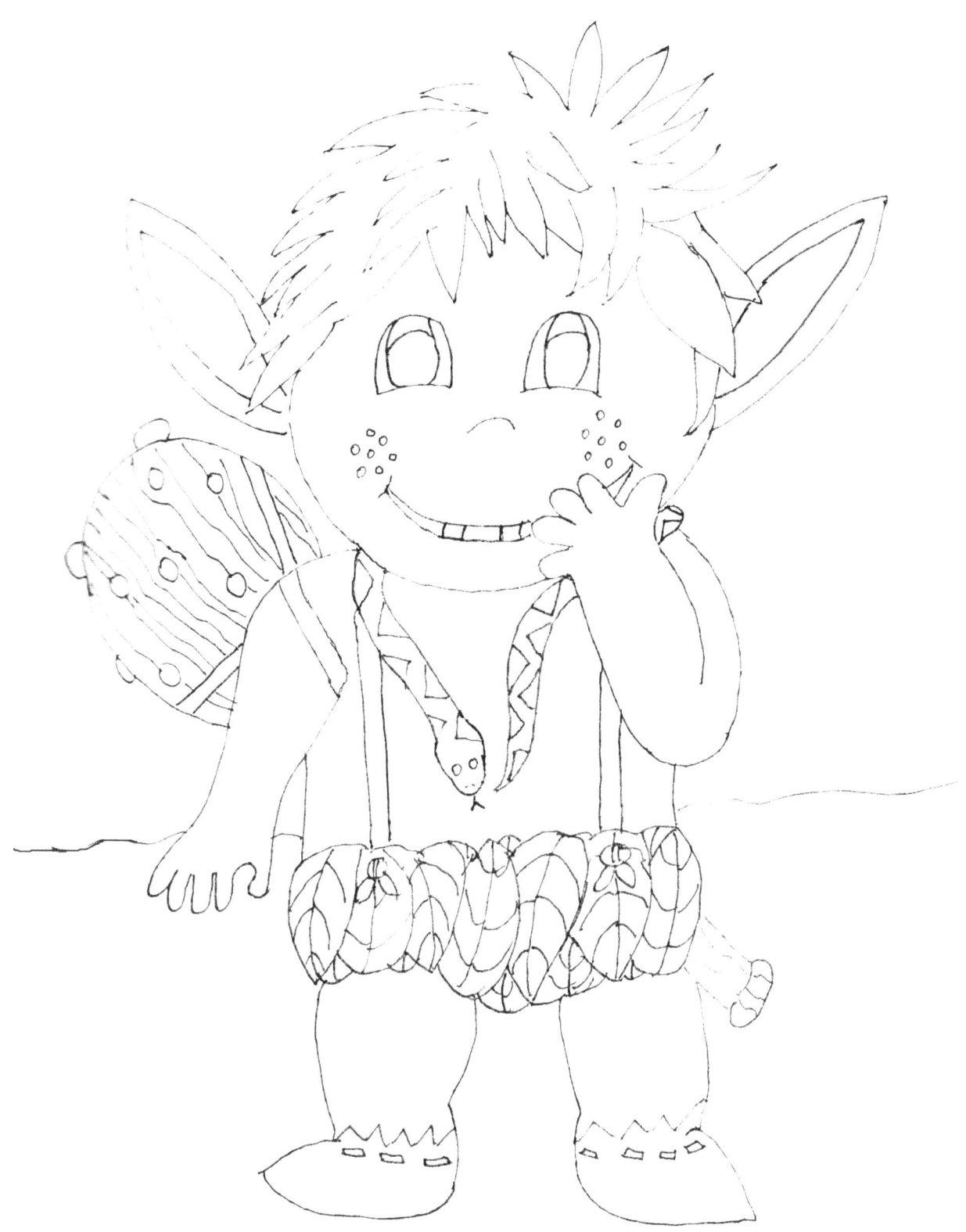

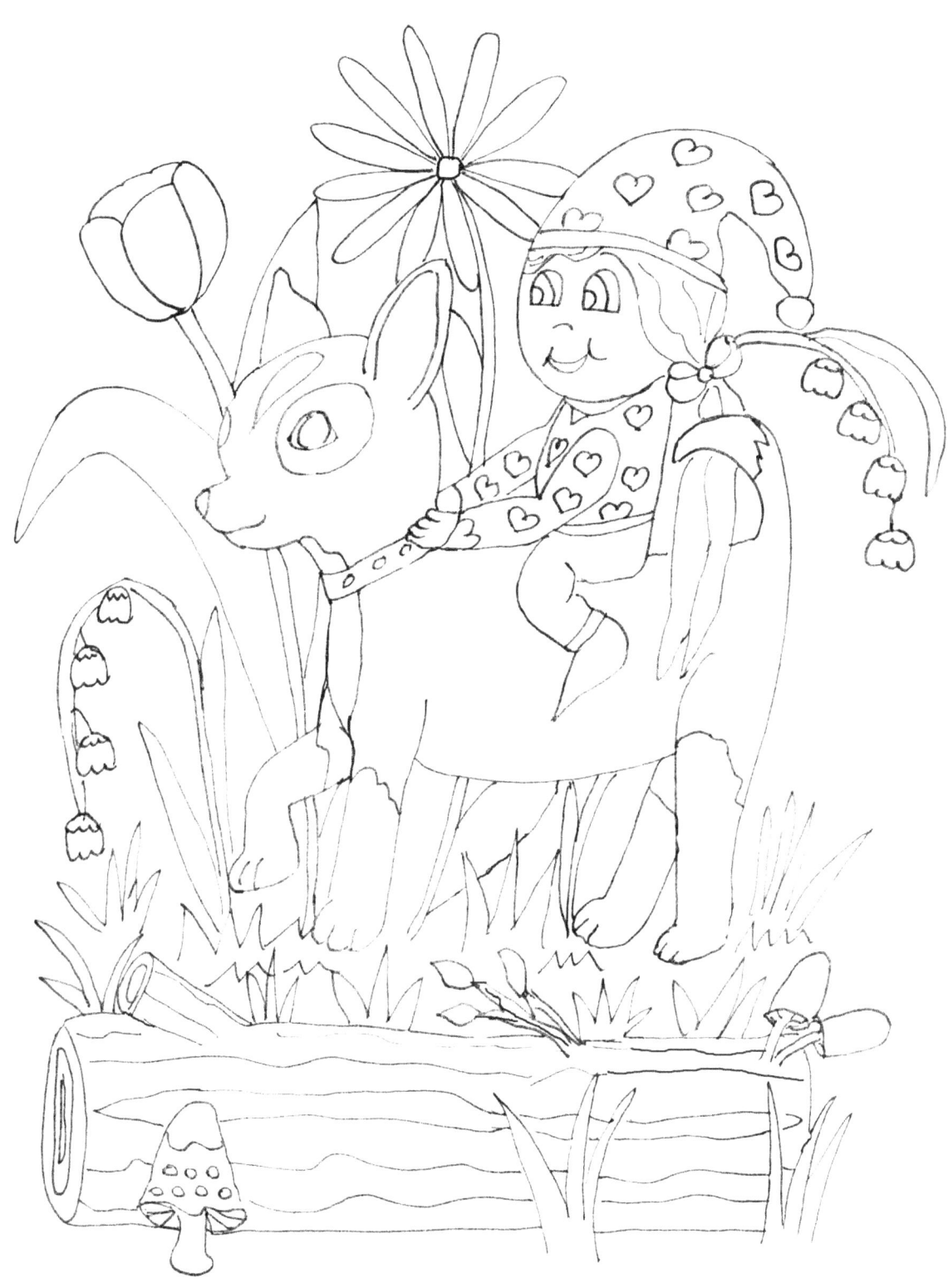

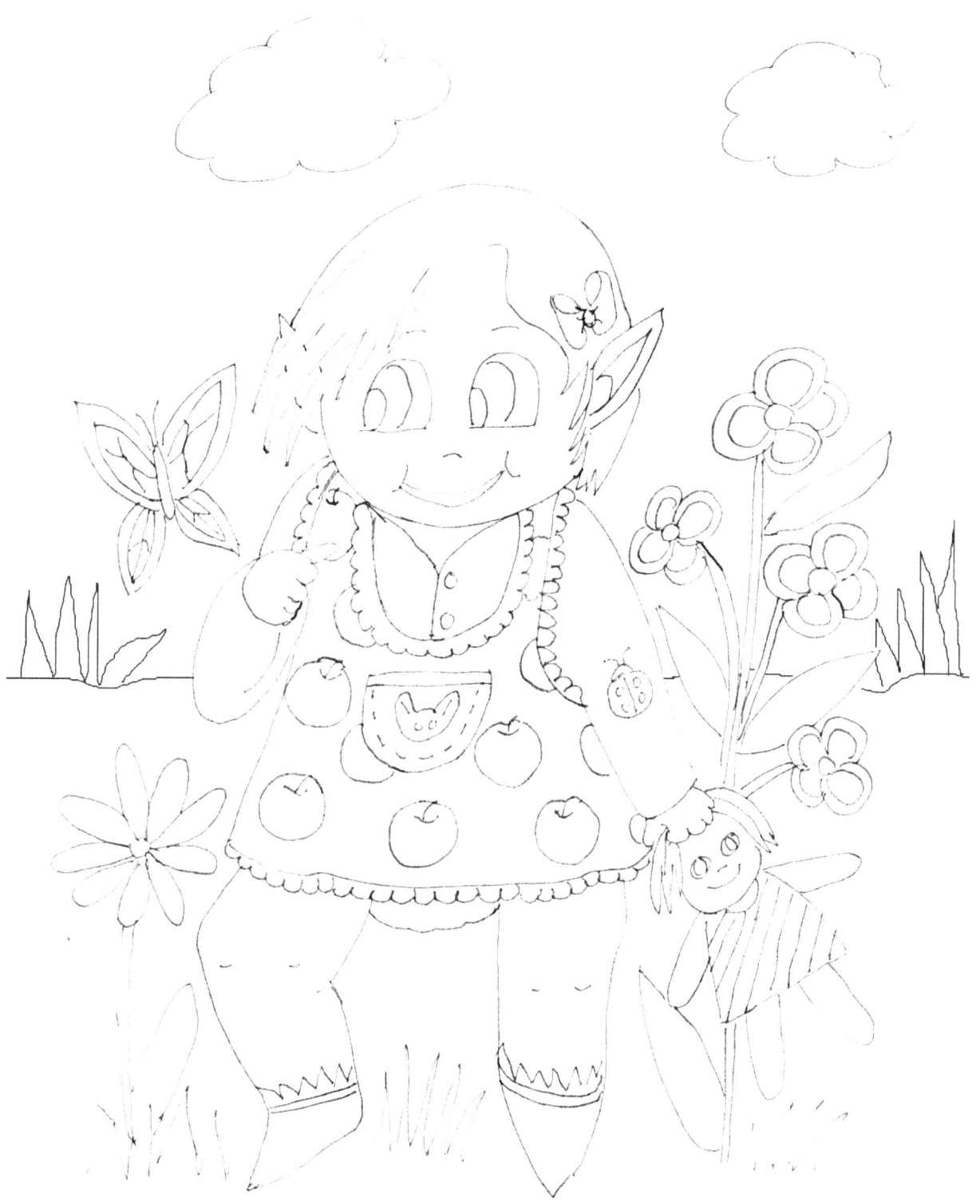

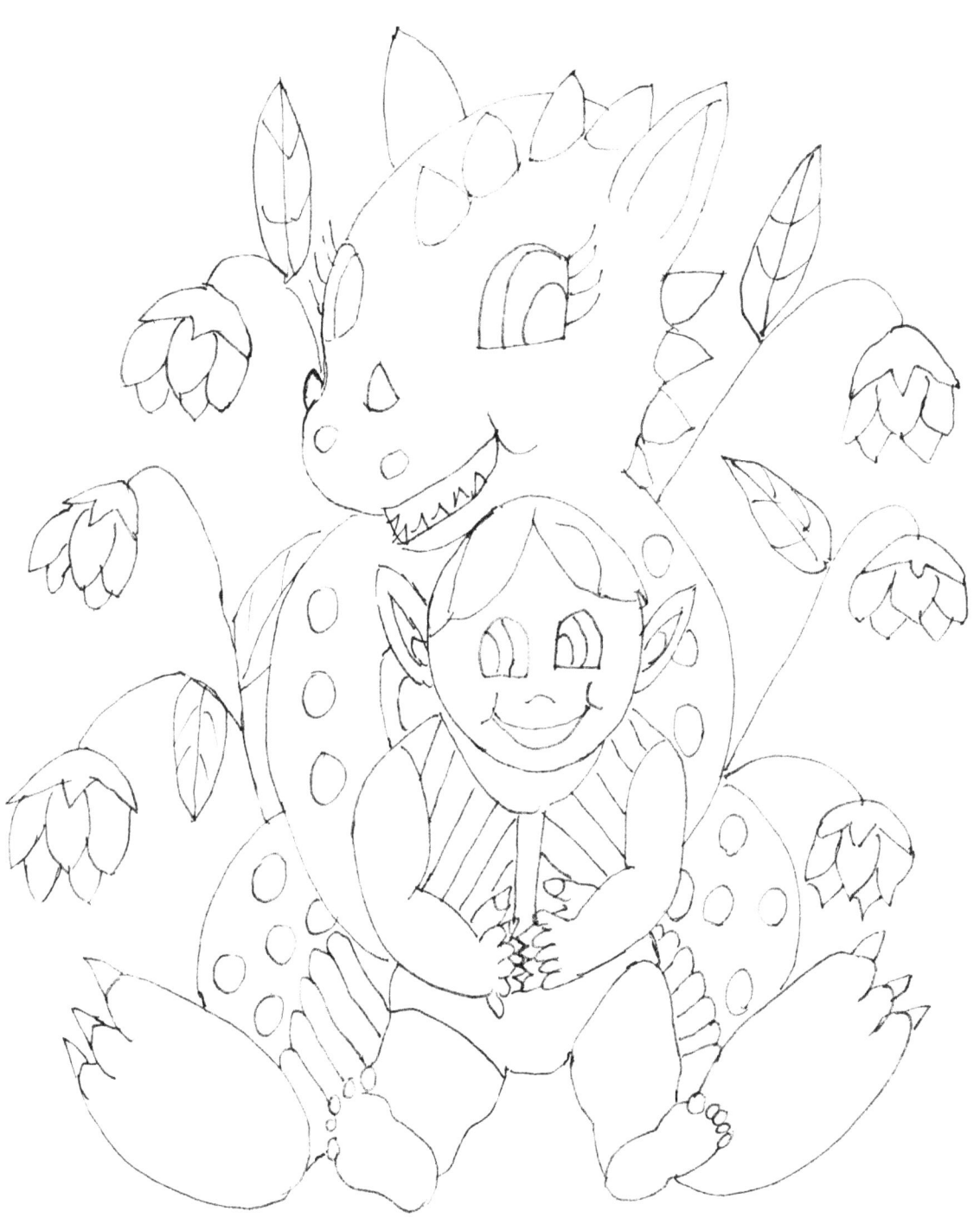

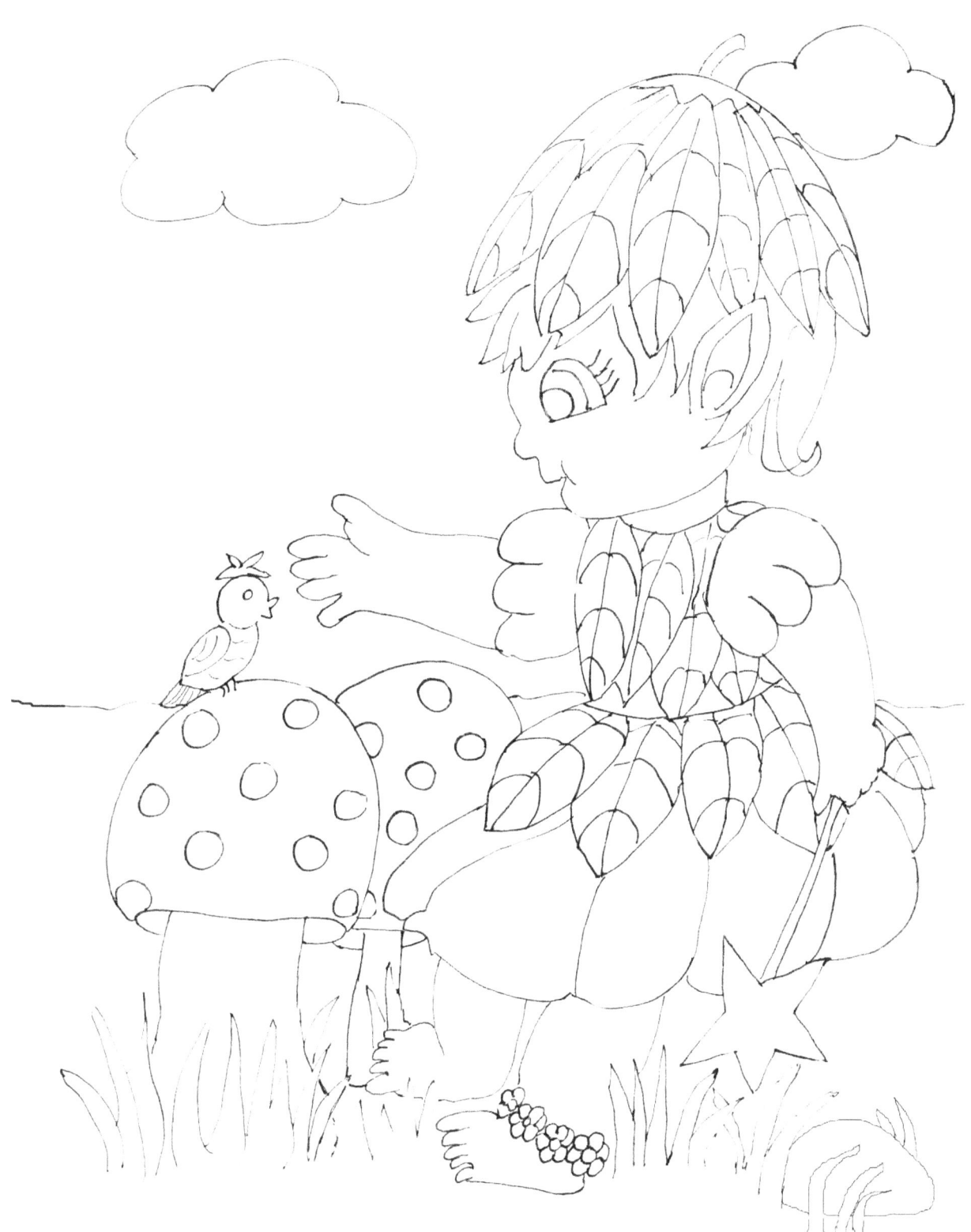

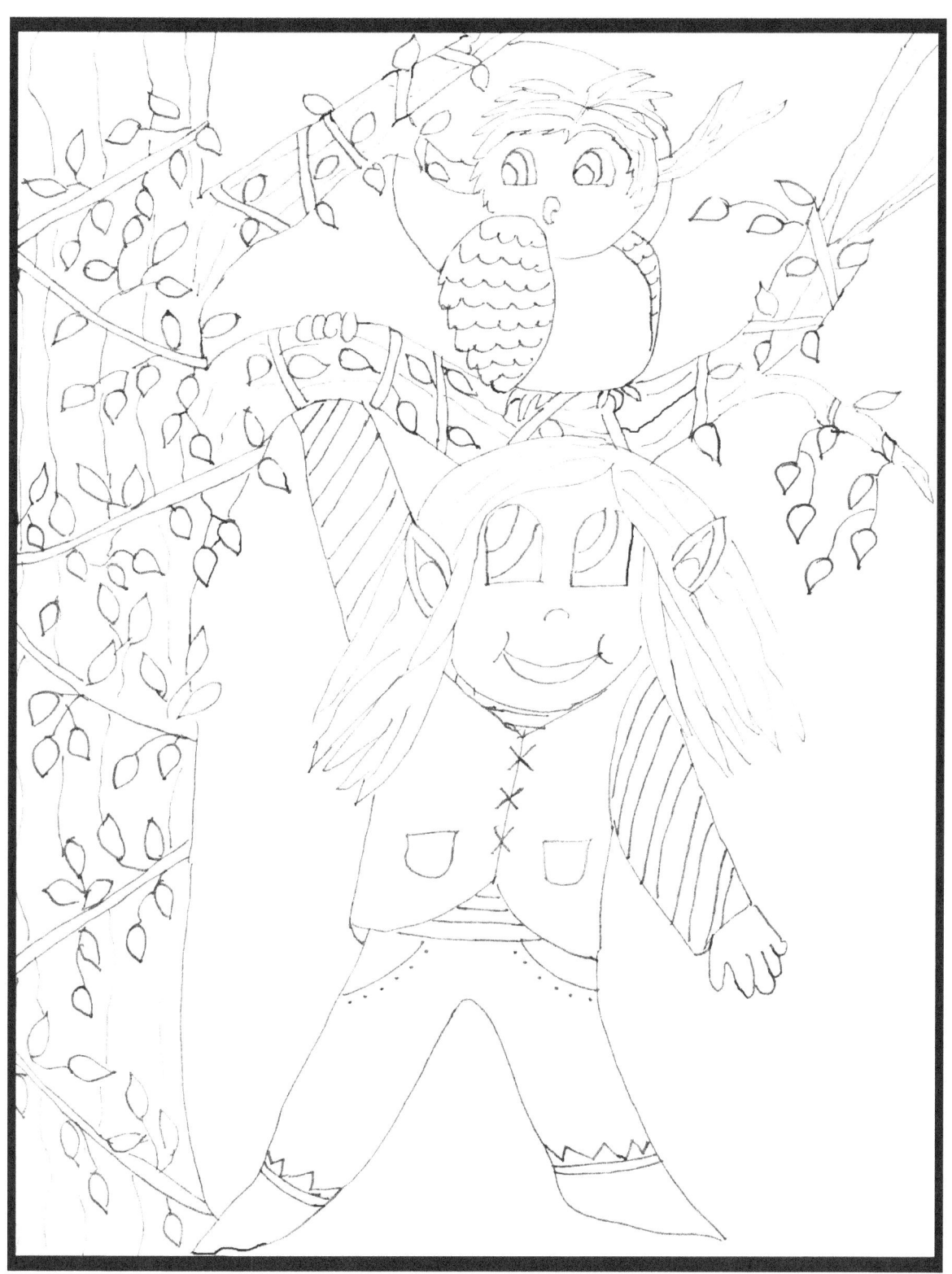

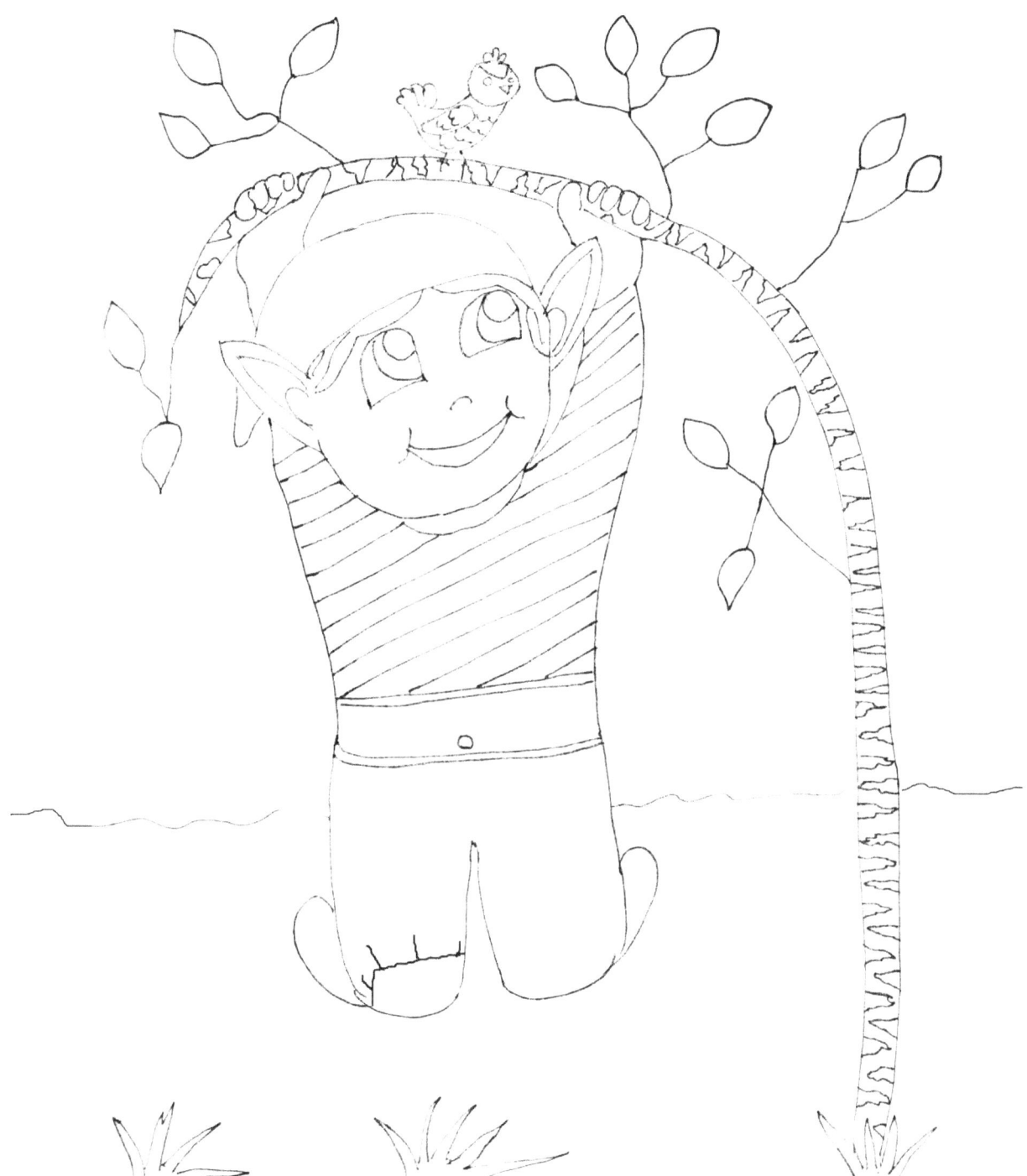

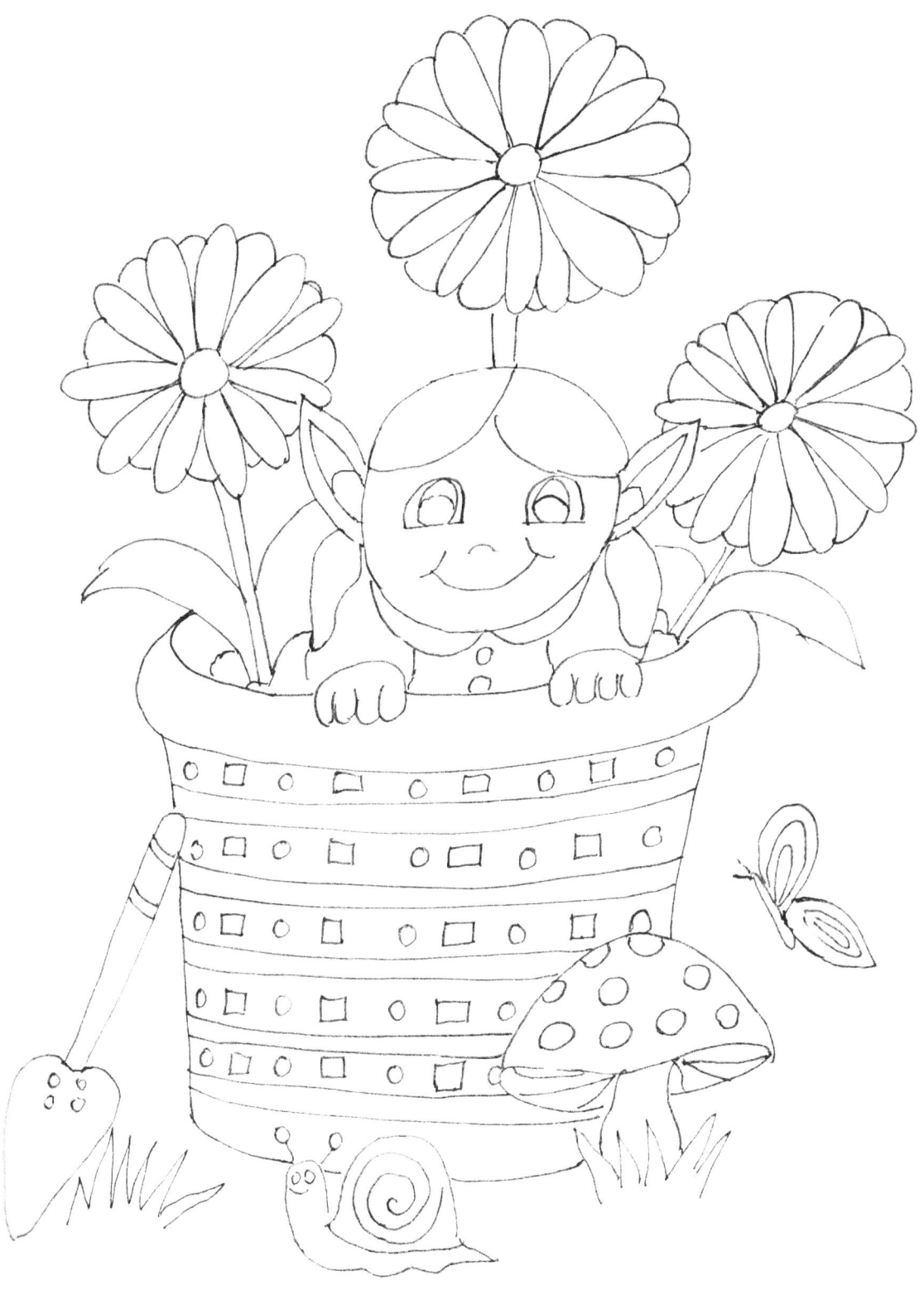

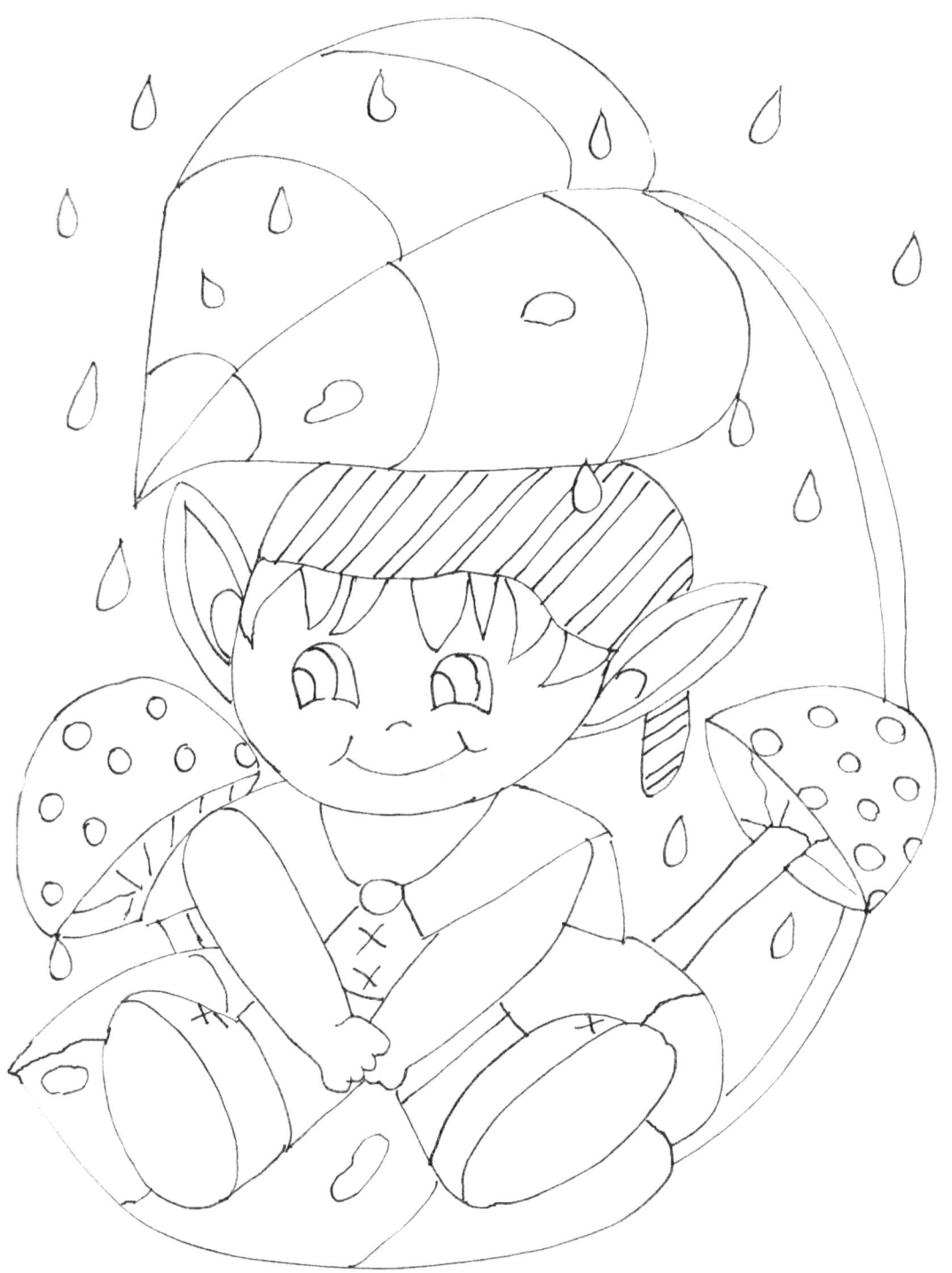

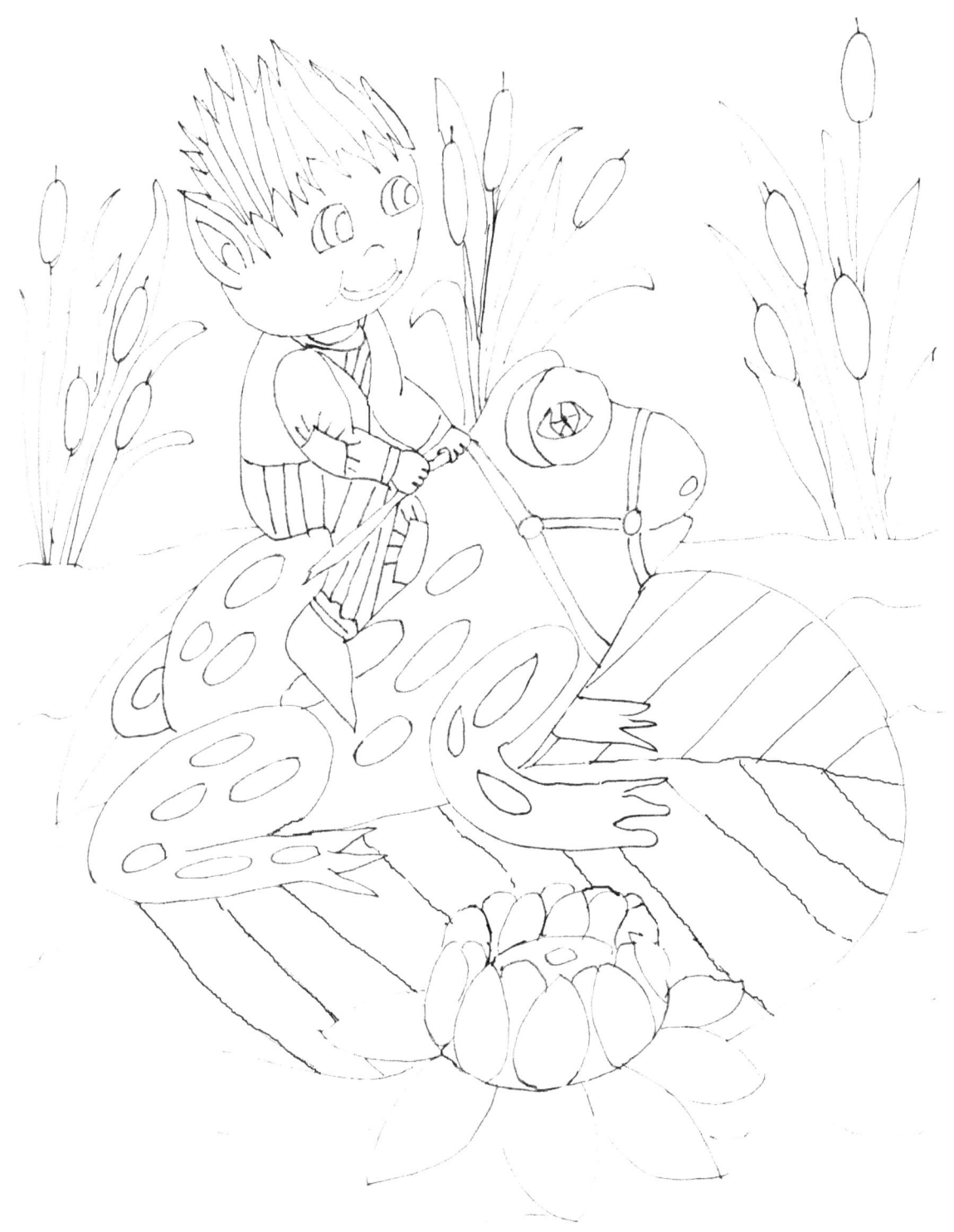

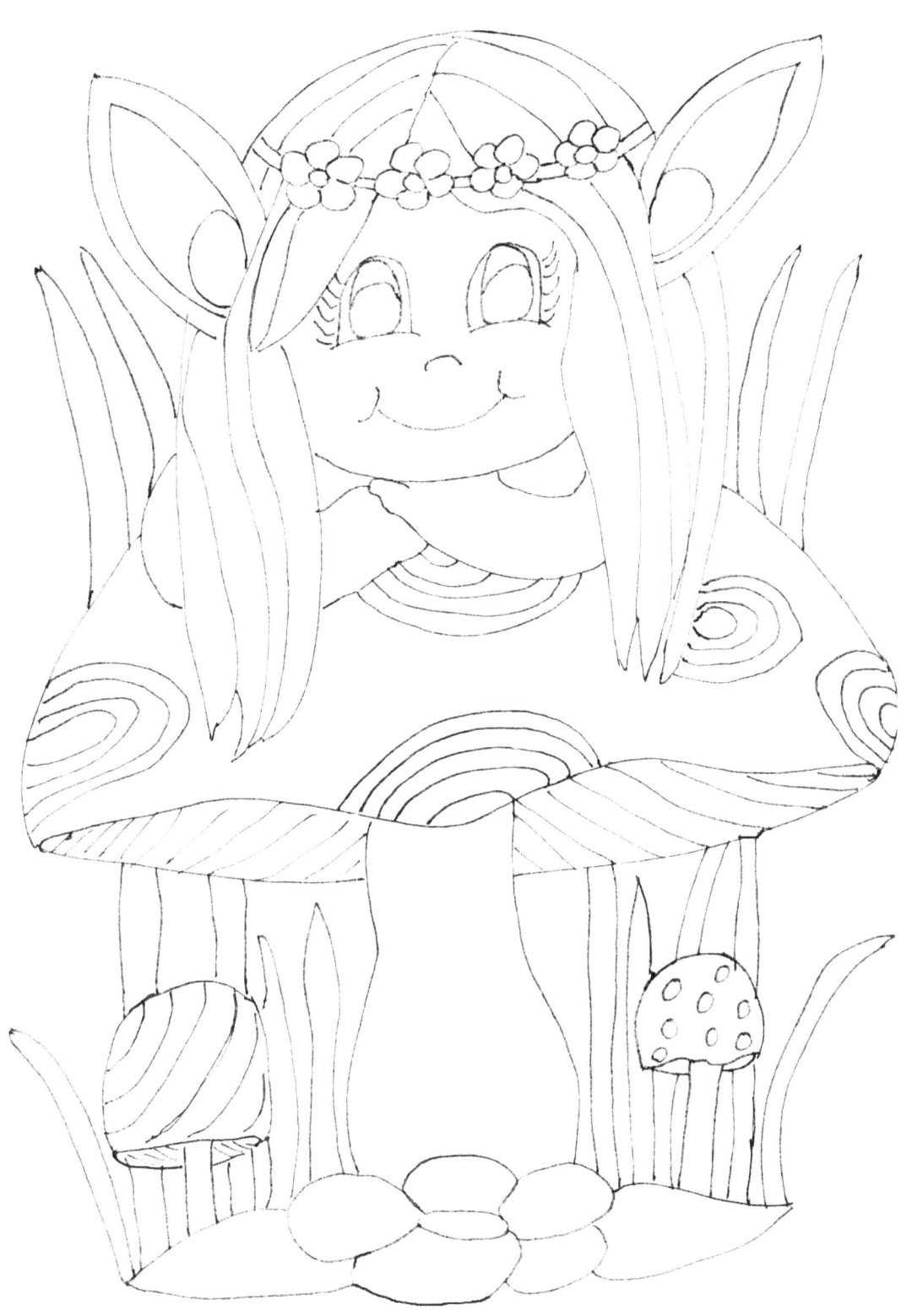

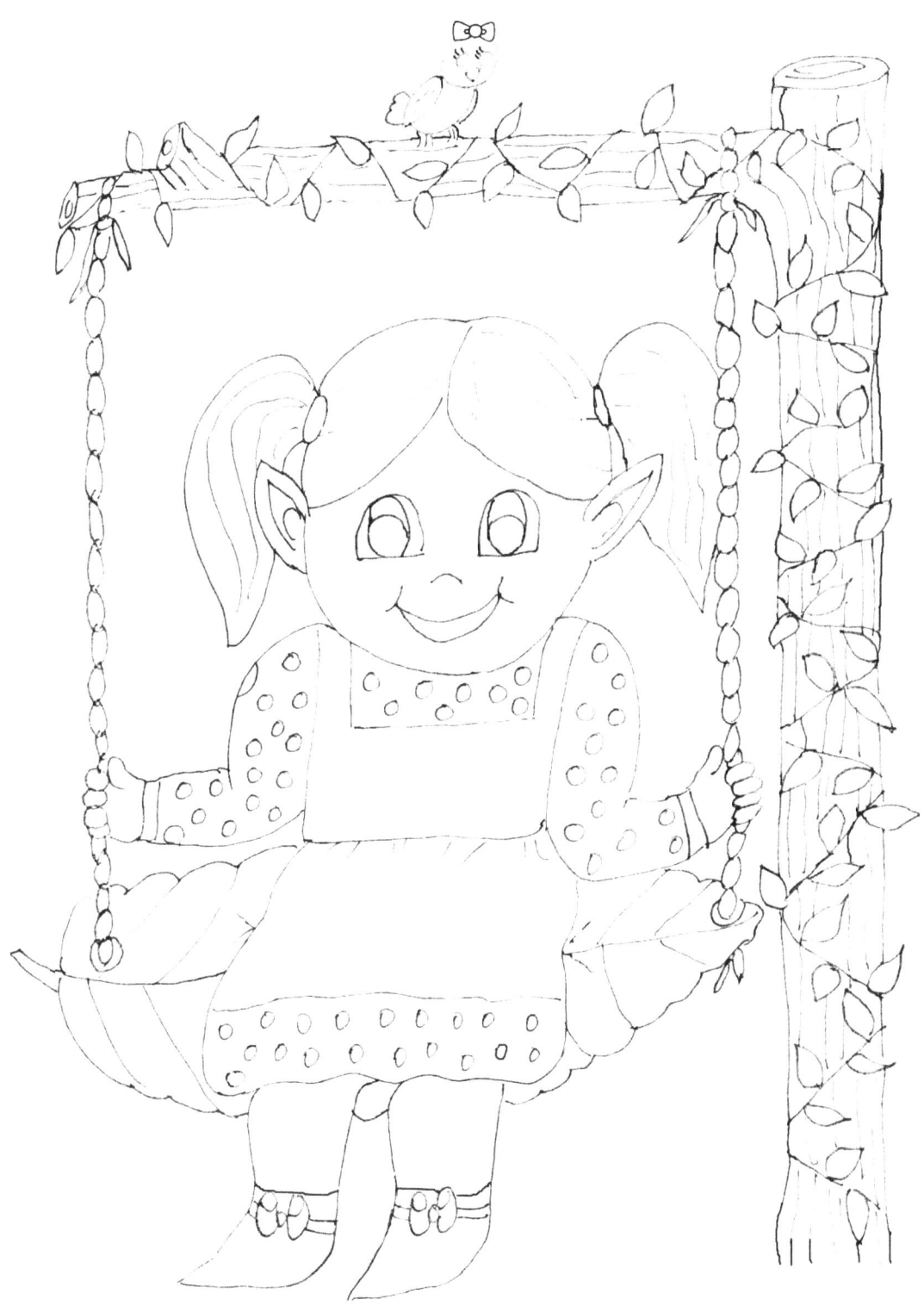

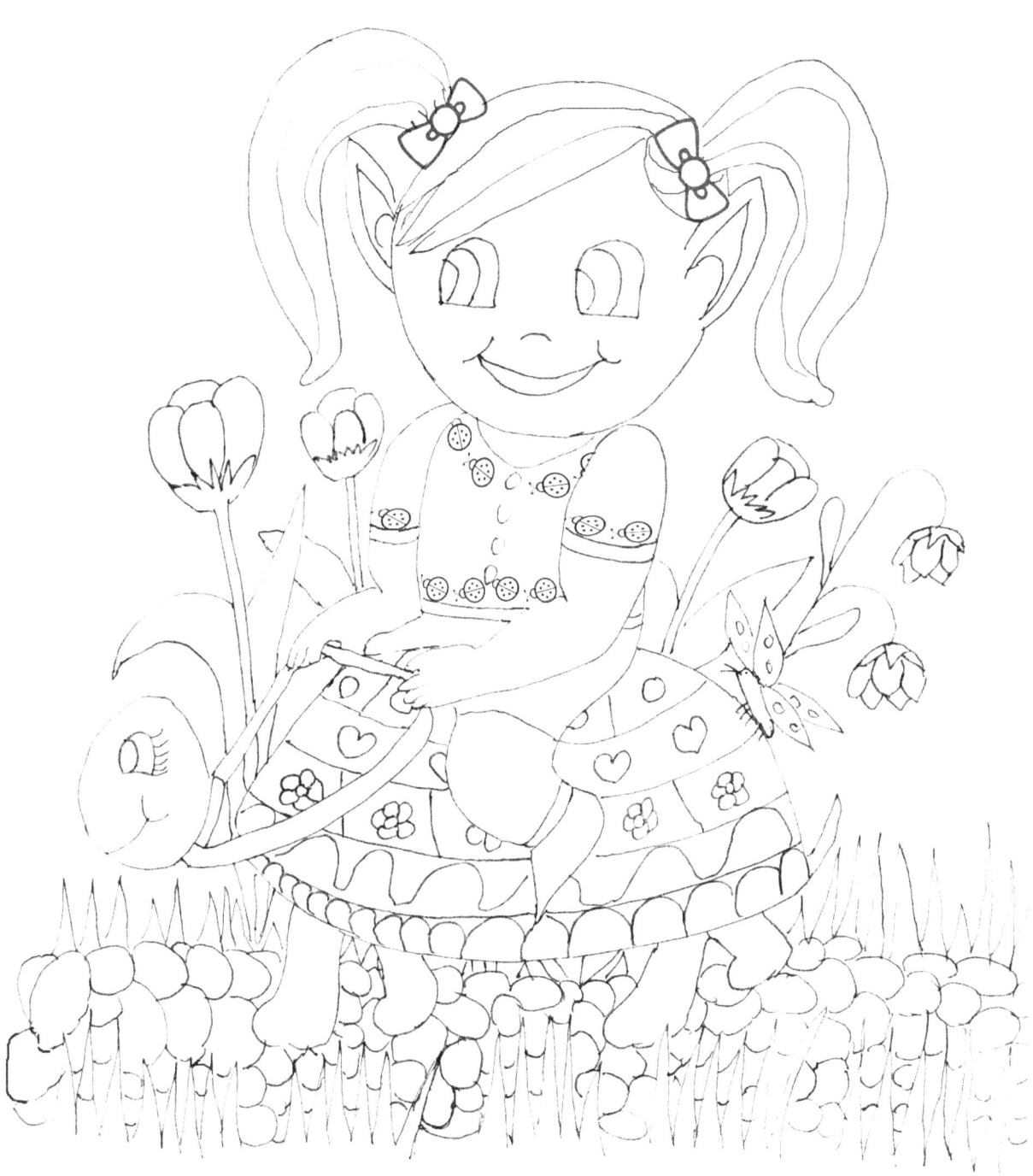

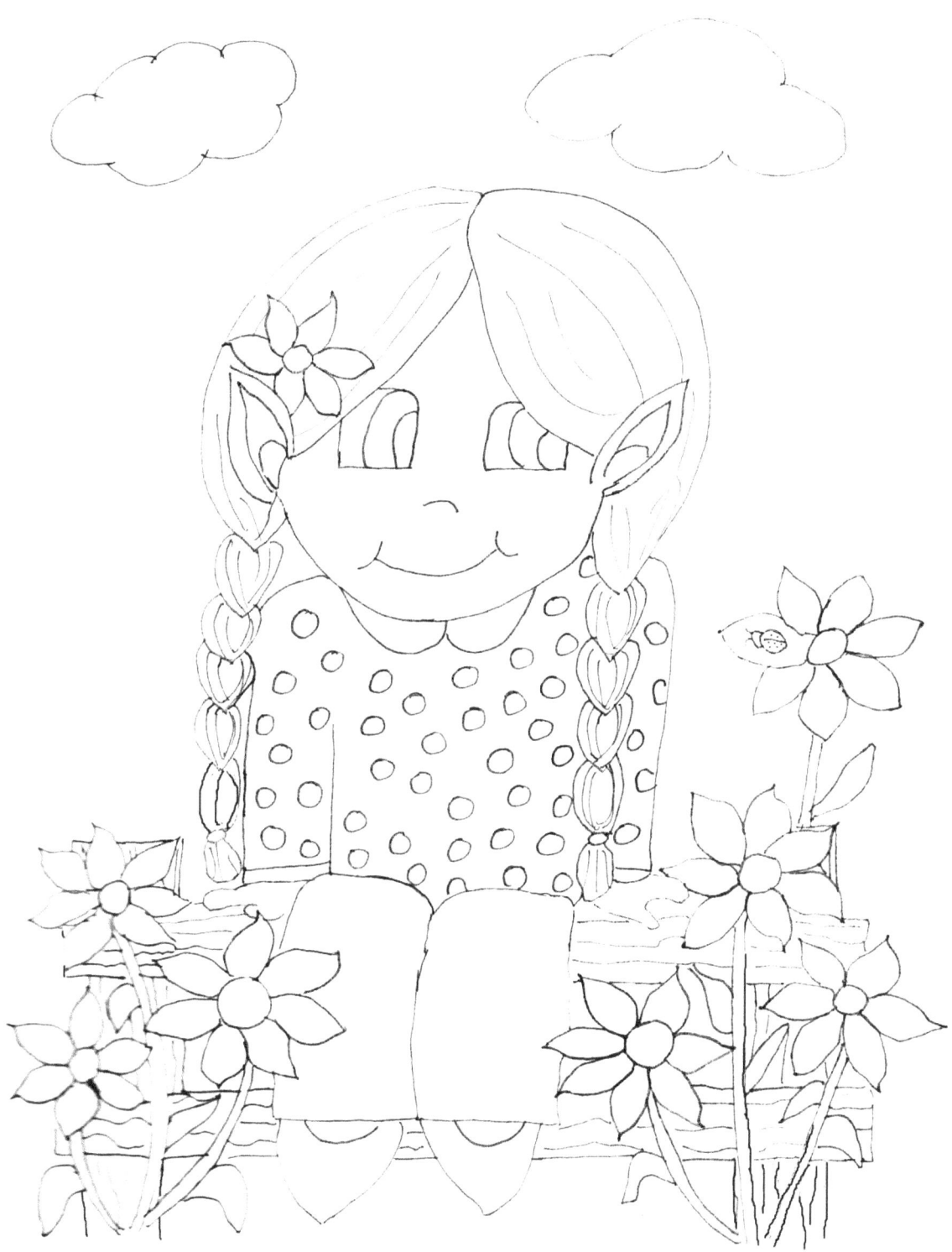

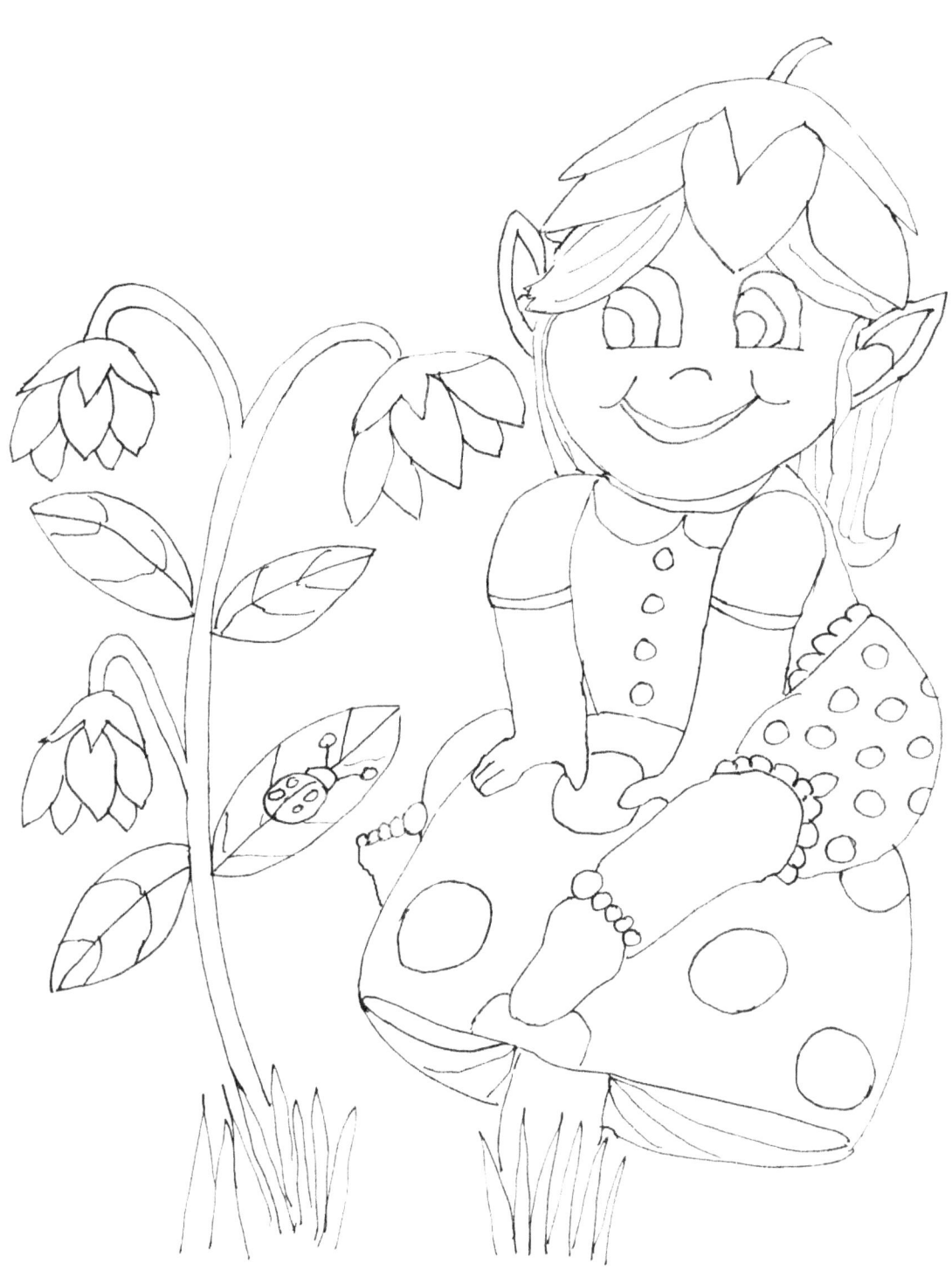

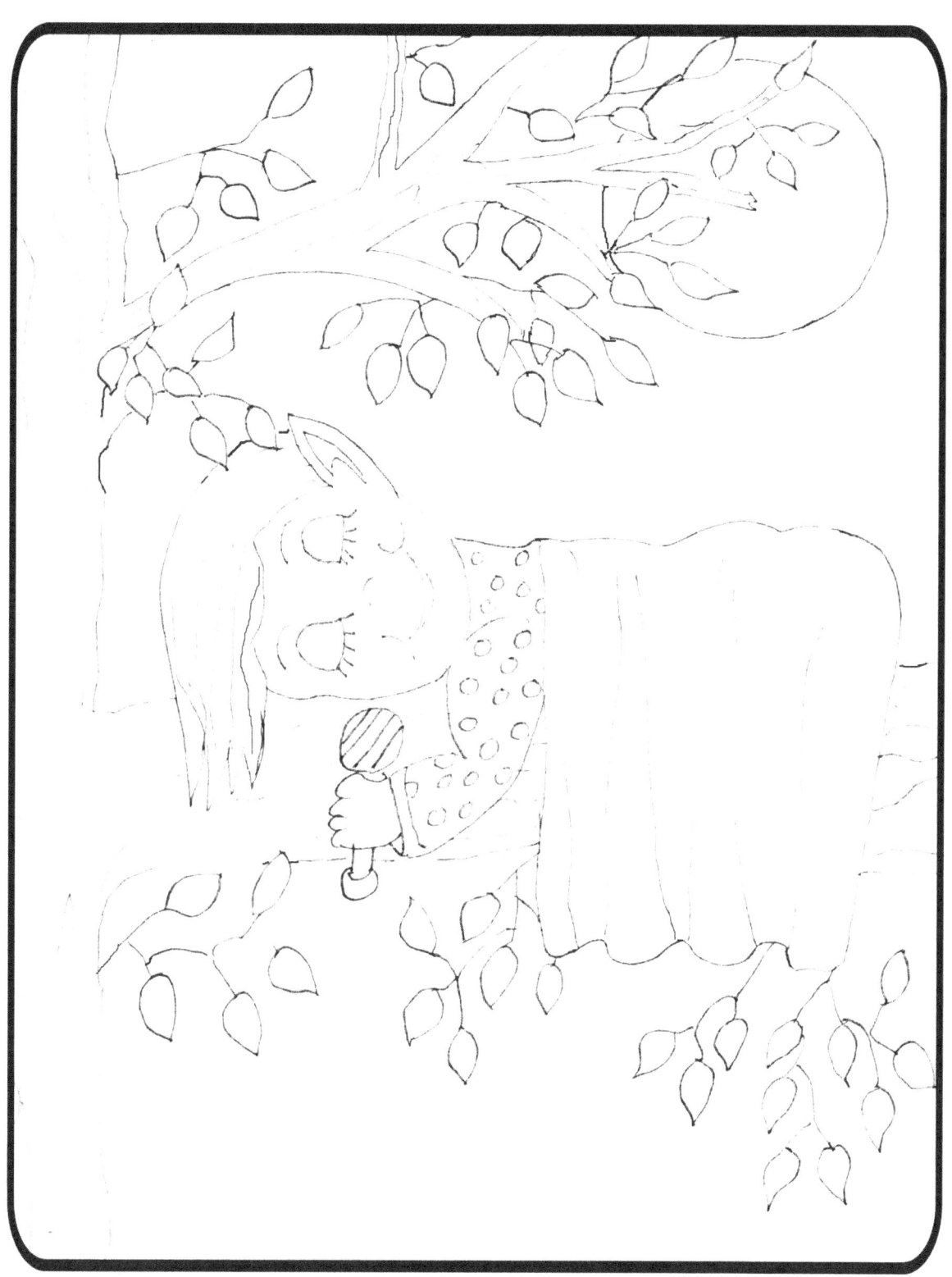

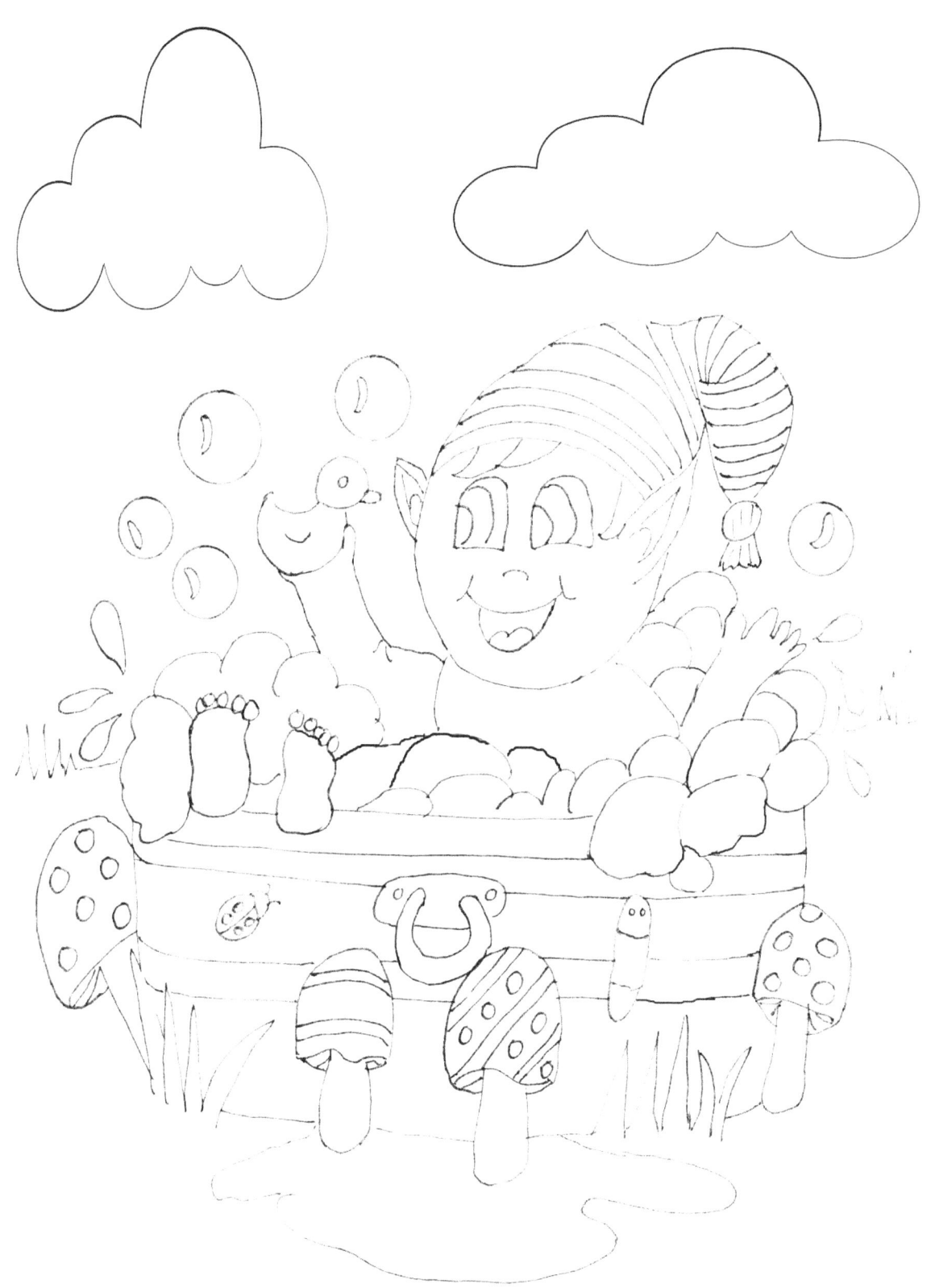

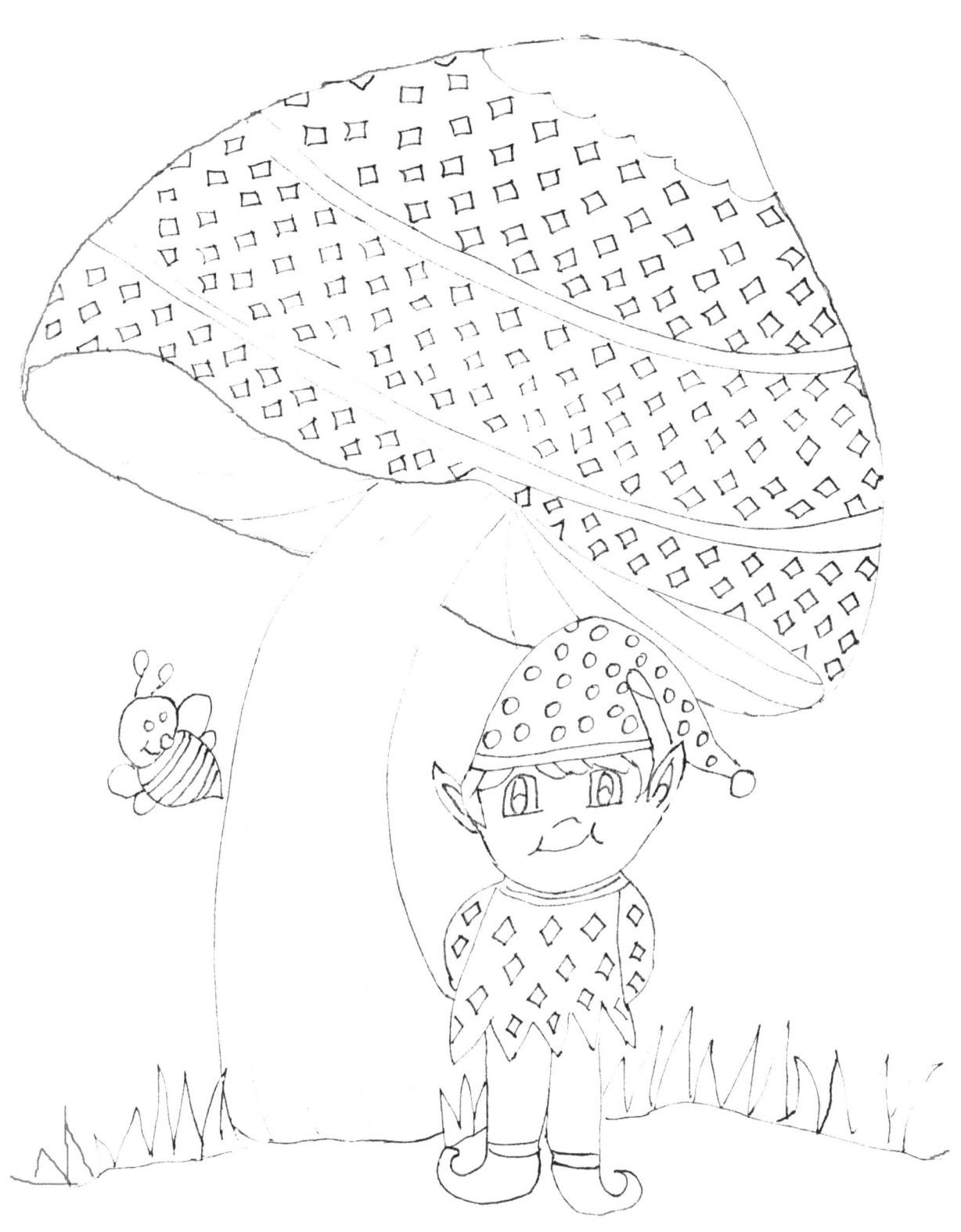

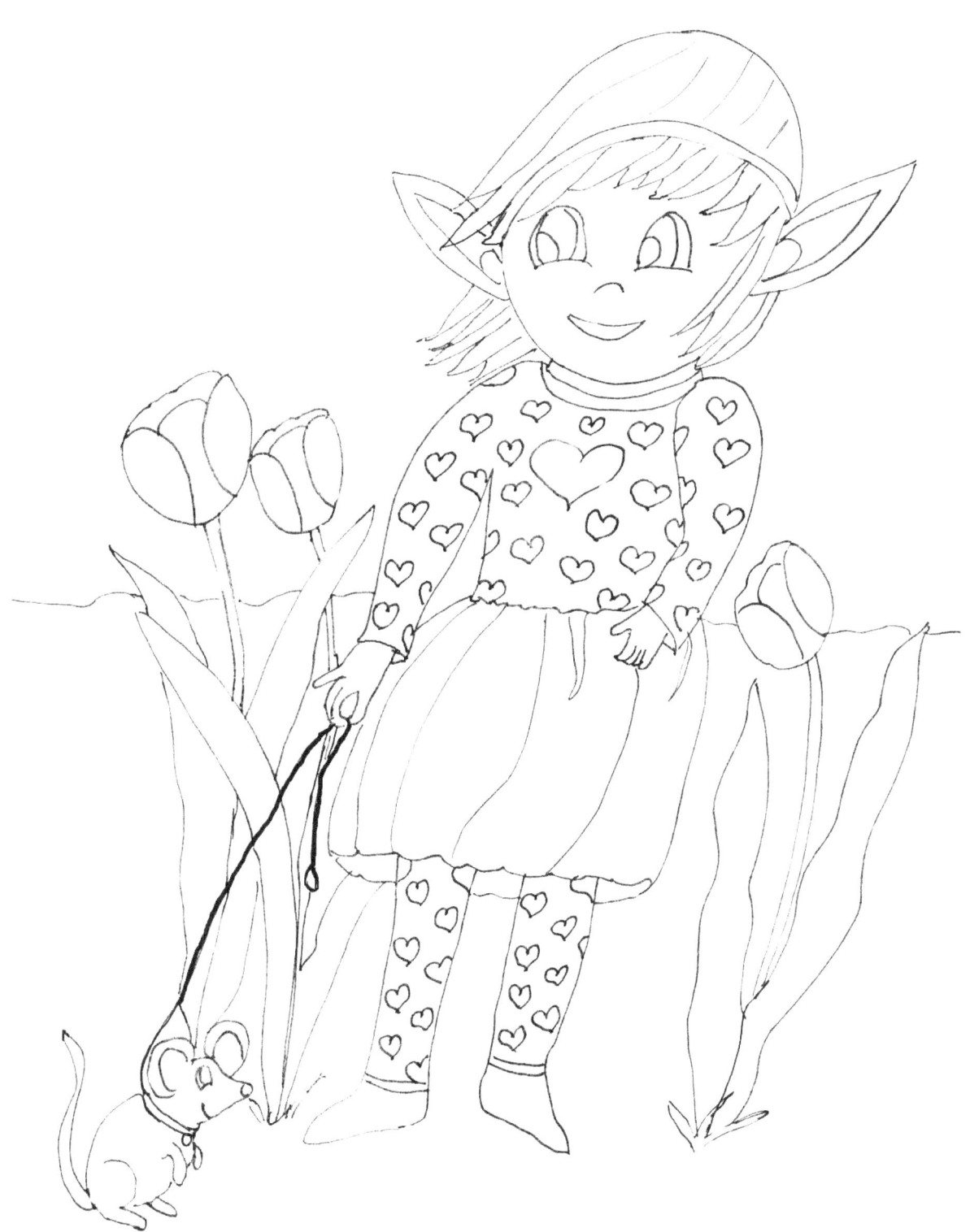

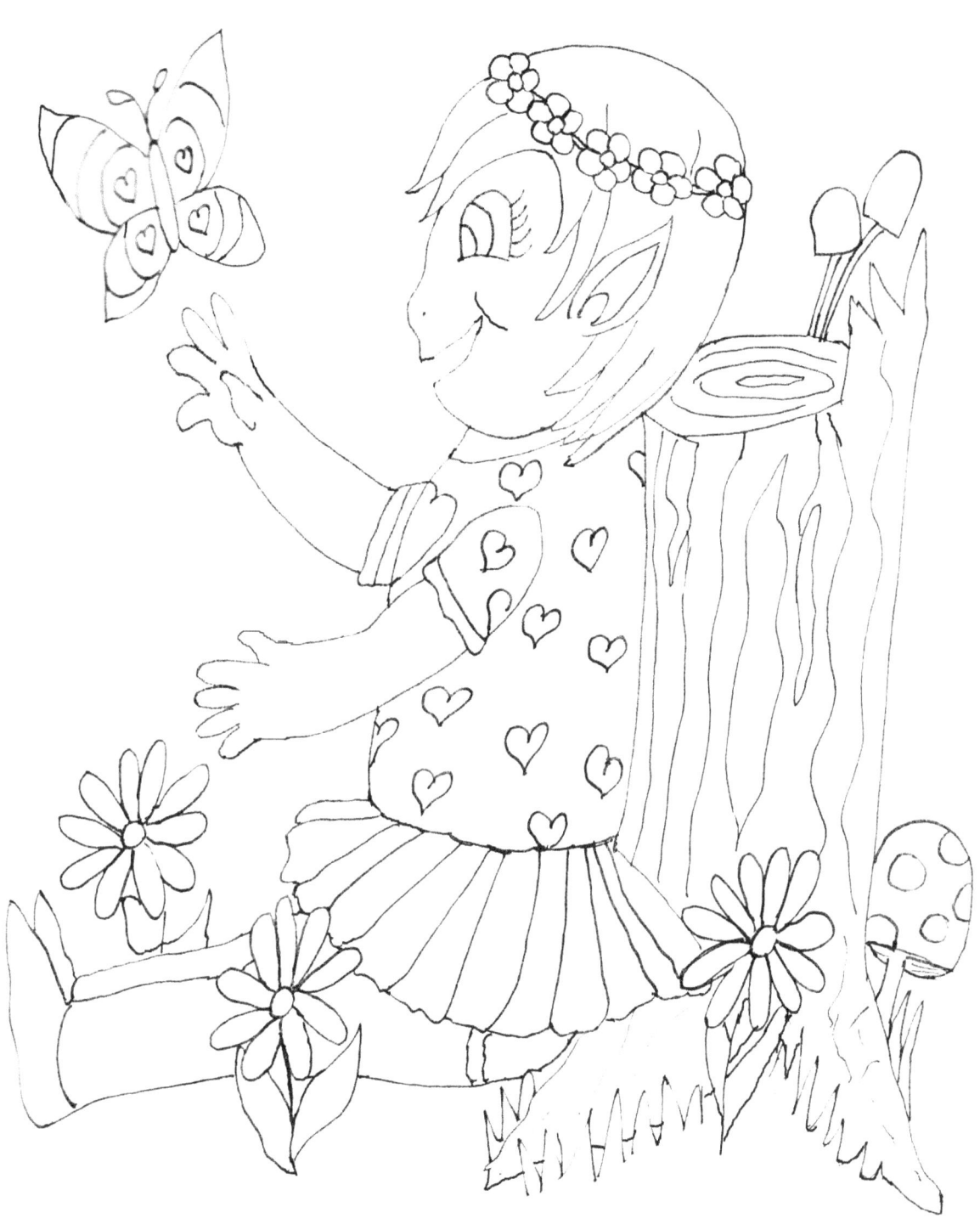

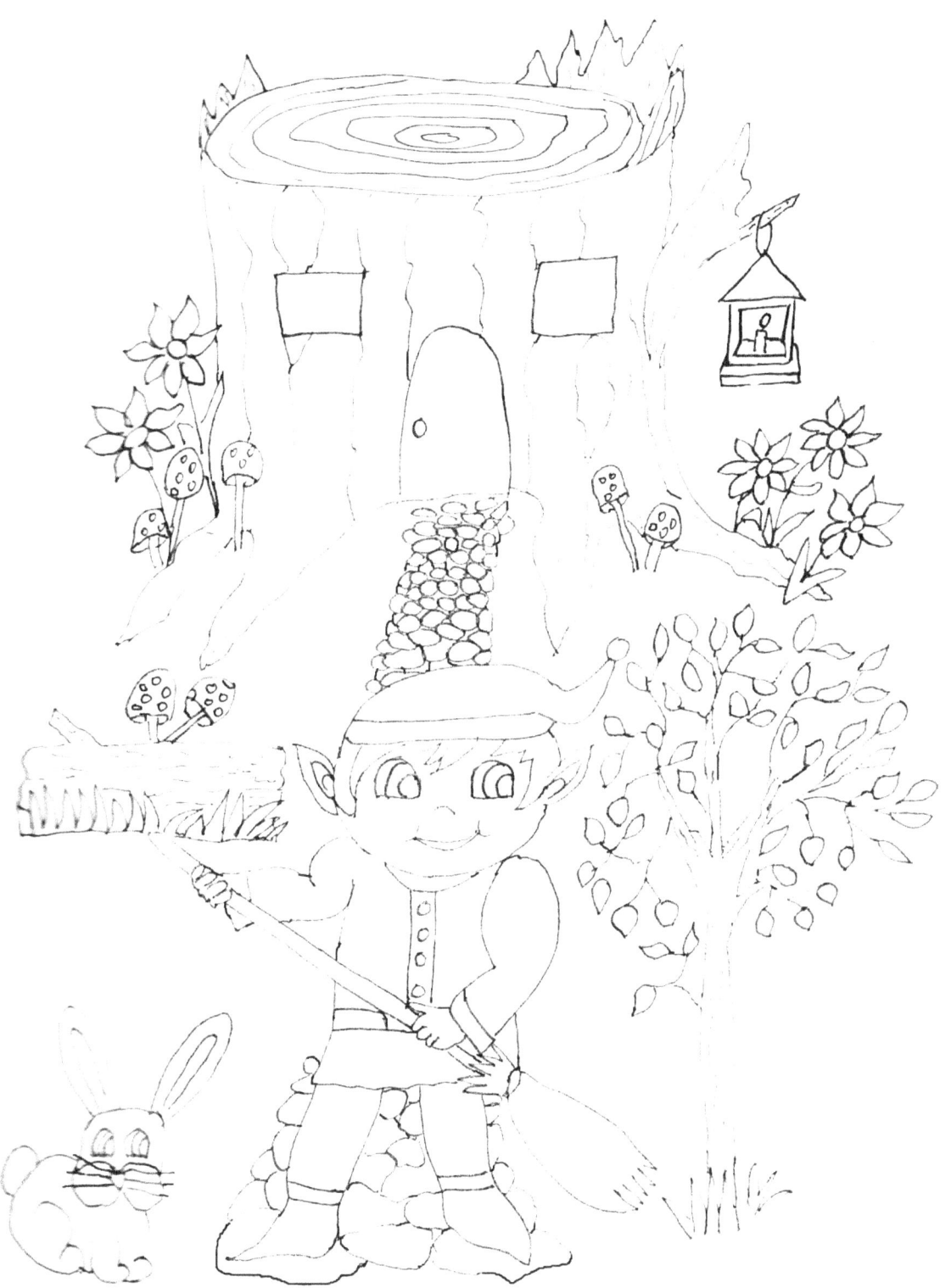

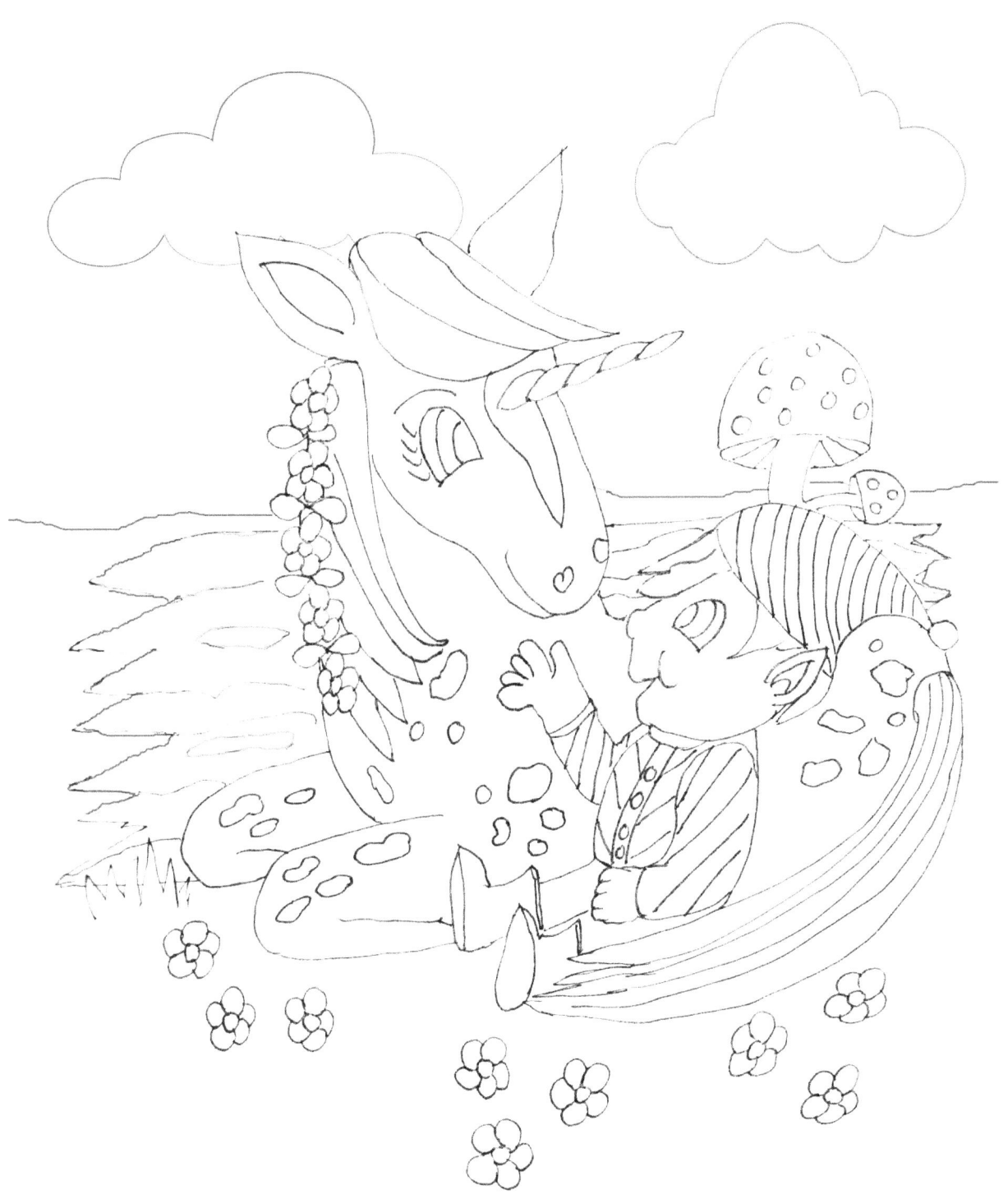

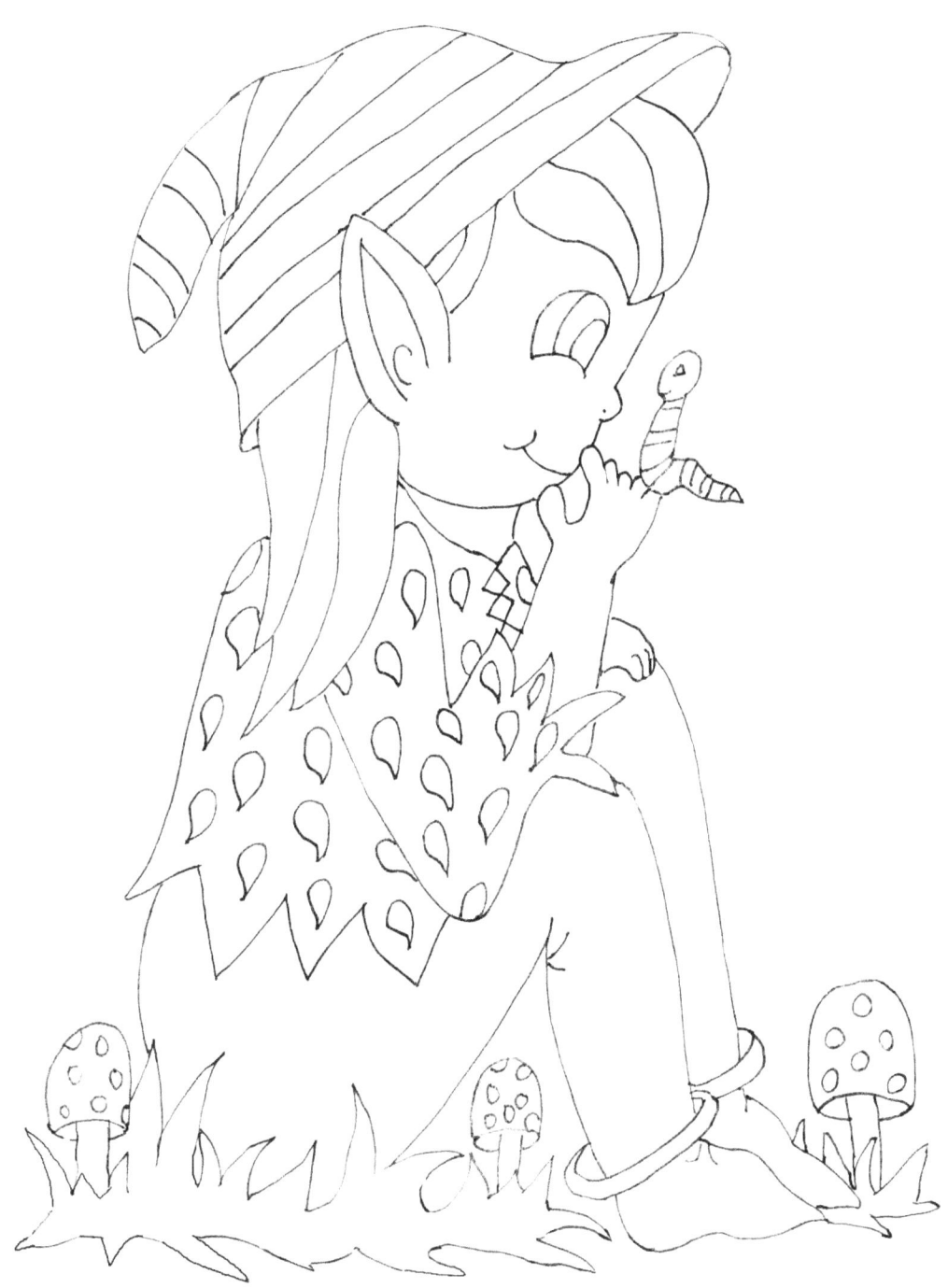

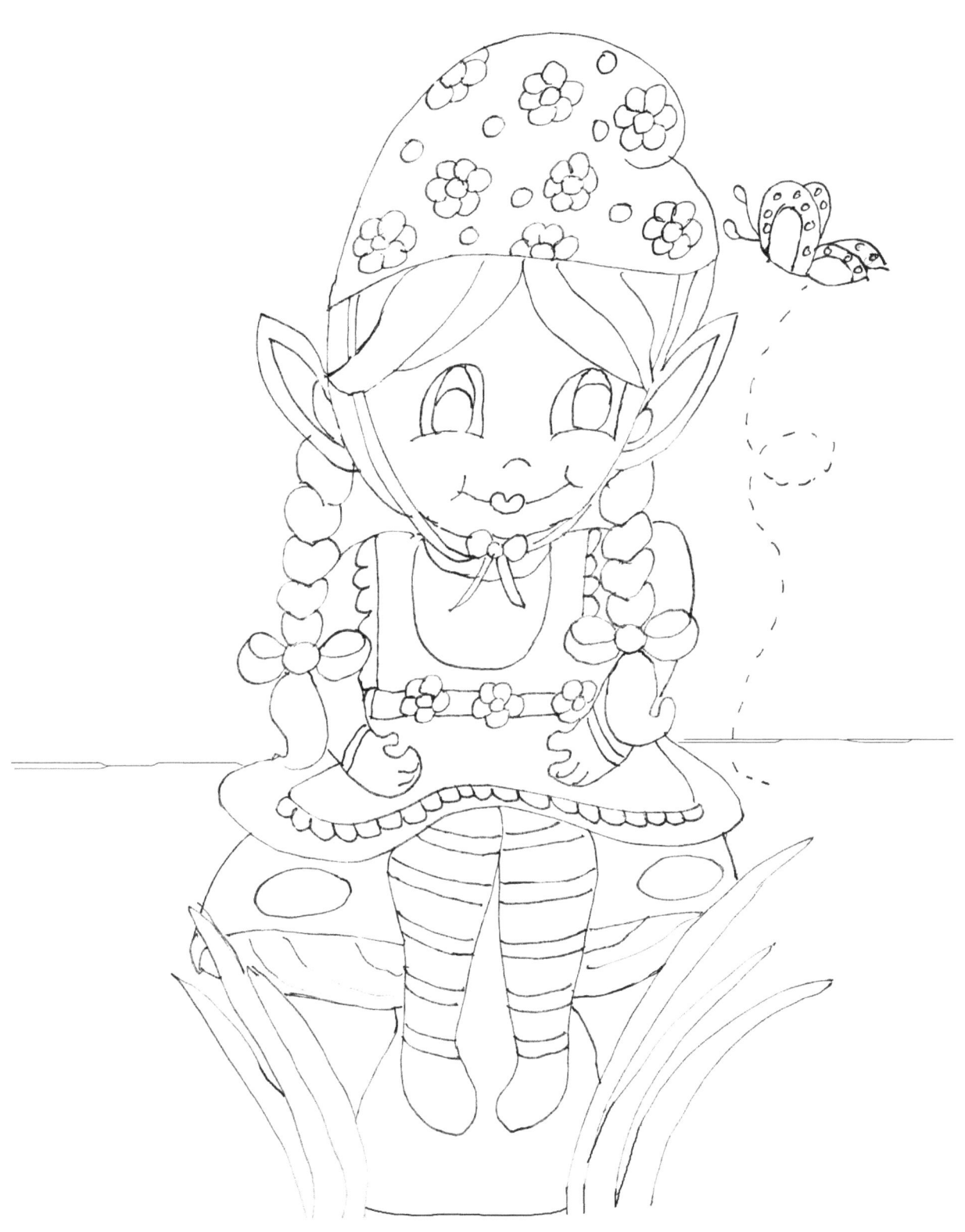

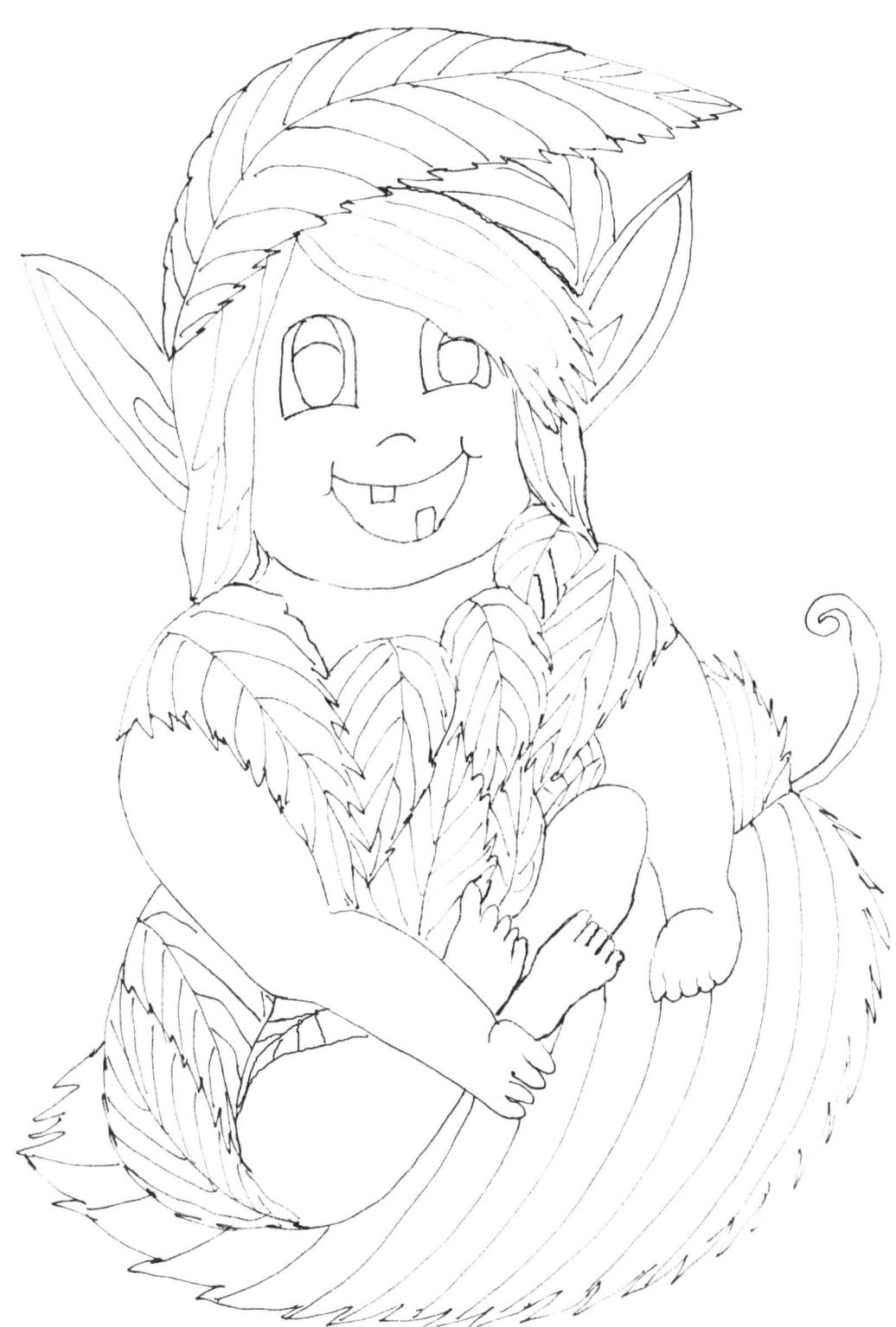

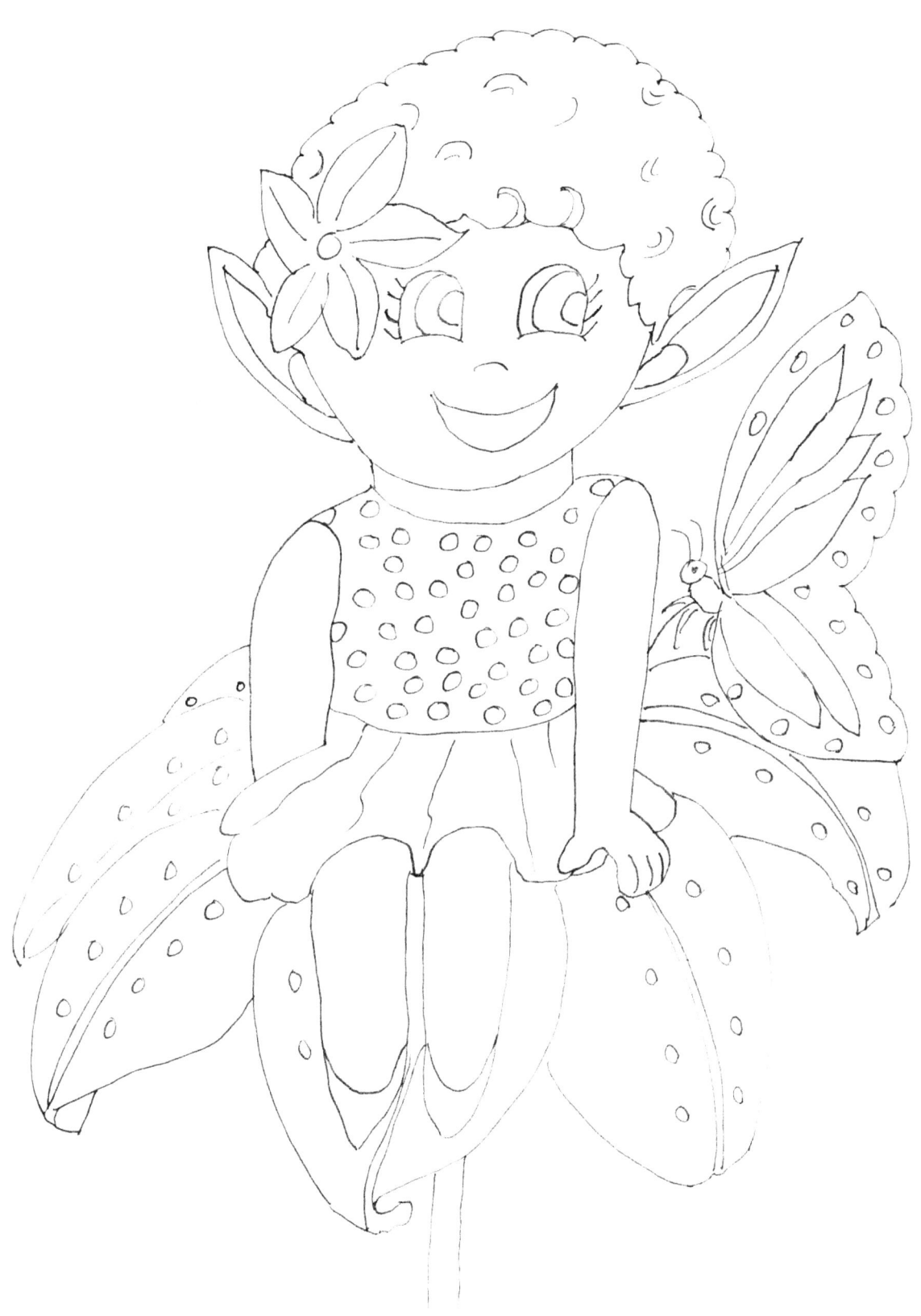

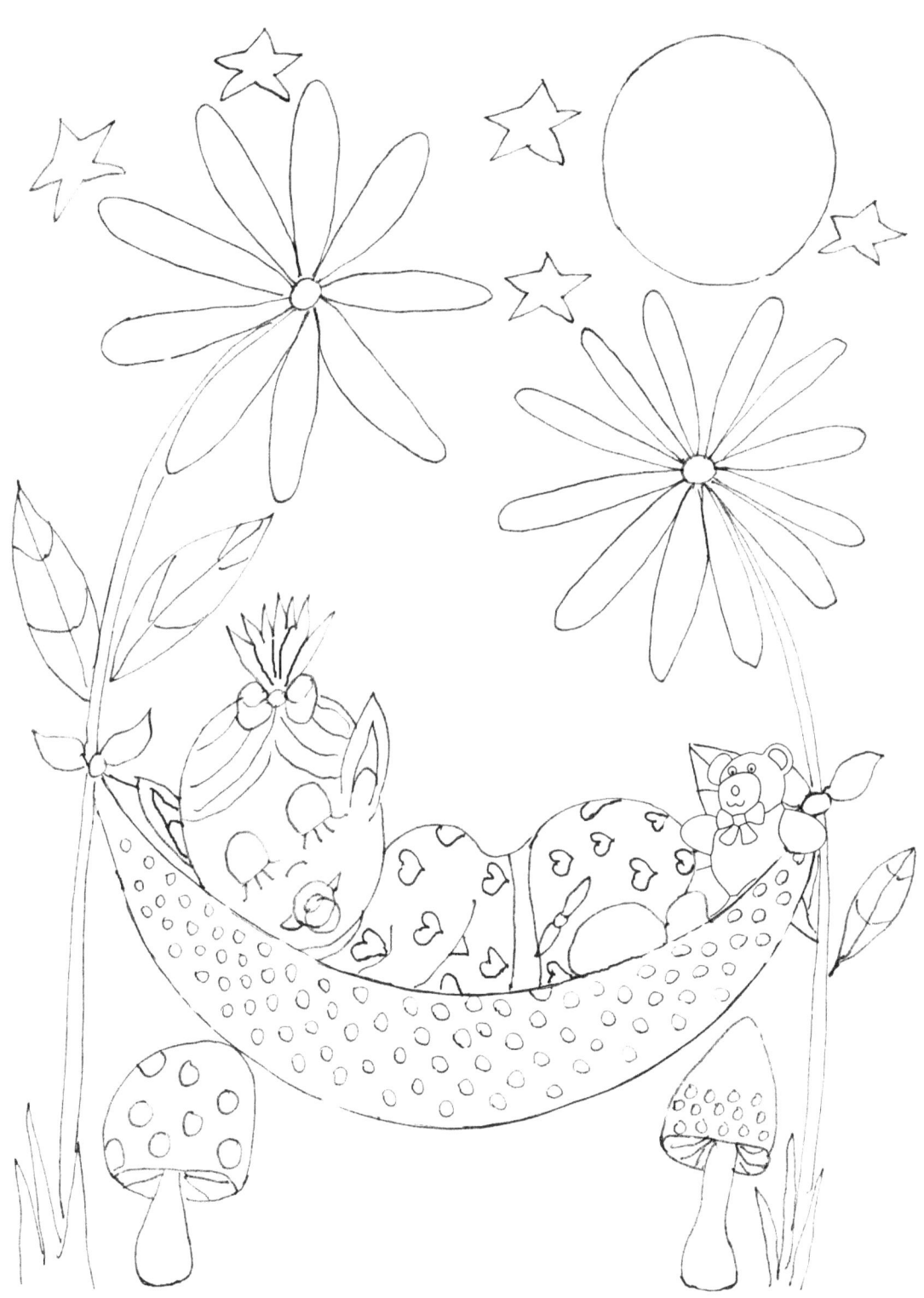

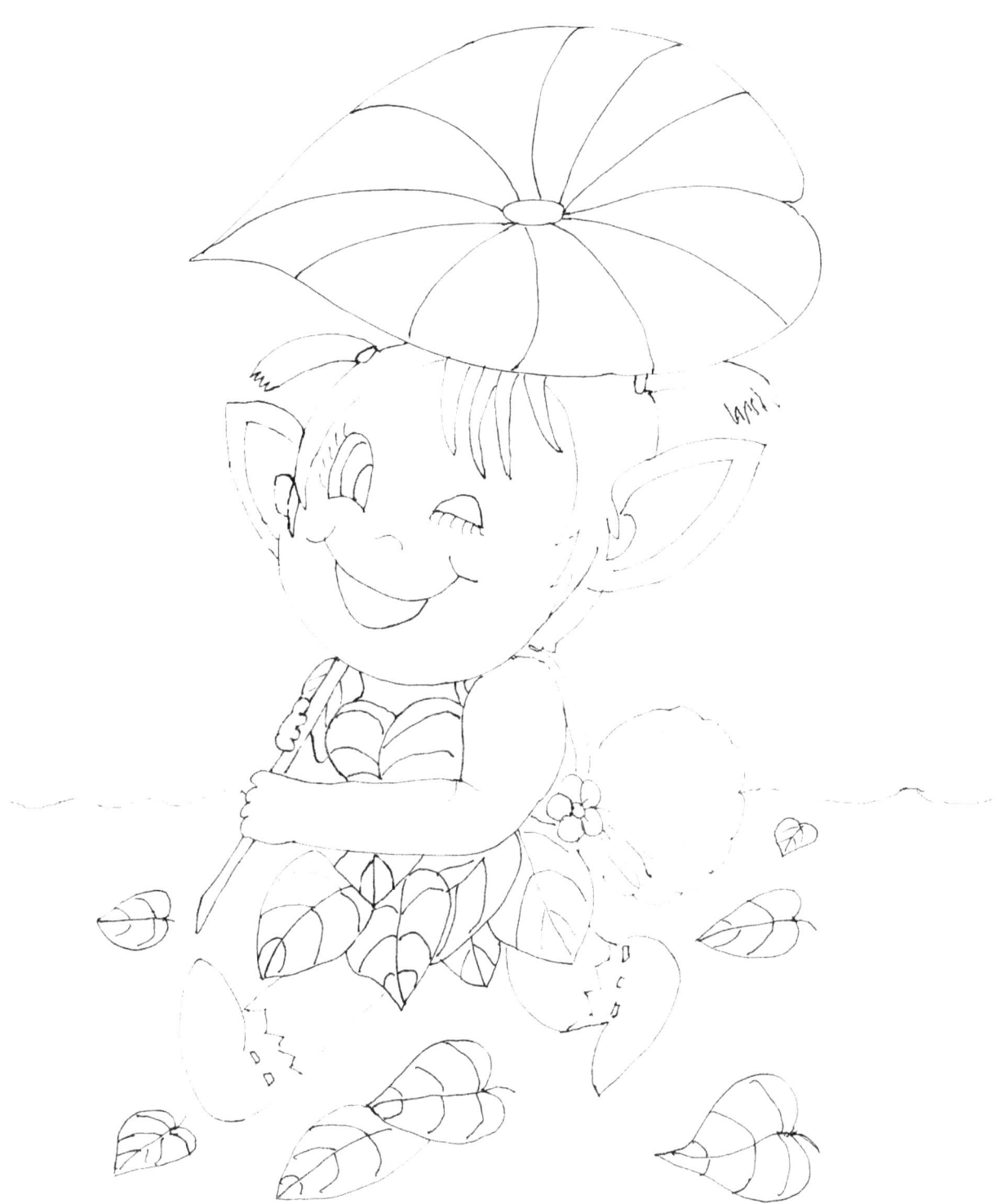

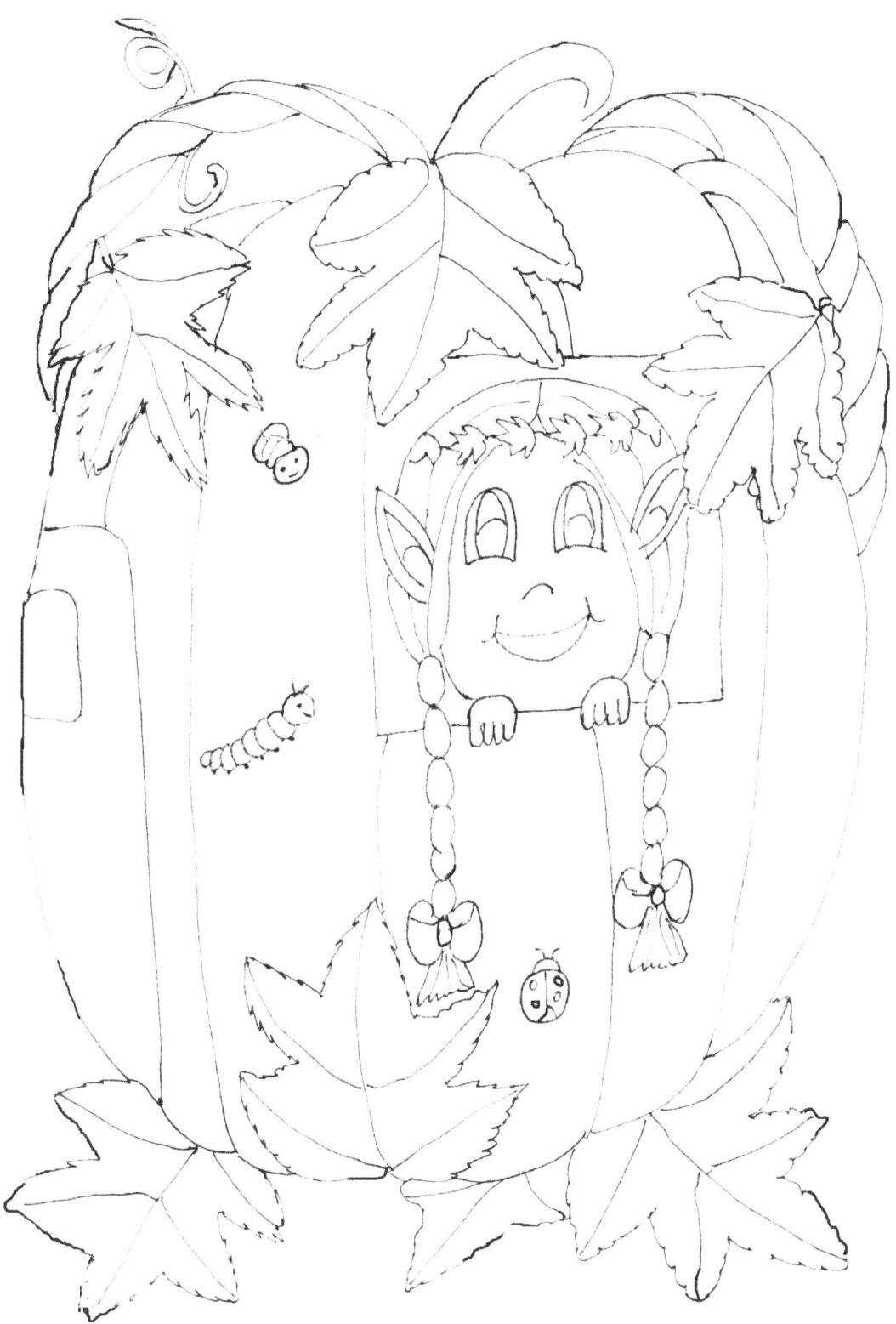

www.ingramcontent.com/pod-product-compliance
Lightning Source LLC
Chambersburg PA
CBHW080540190526
45169CB00007B/2569